Sex and Psychic Energy

Beyond the Sexual Revolution

Betty Bethards

Introduction by Cary E. McCarthy, PhD
Illustrations by Leo August

Inner Light Foundation   Novato   California

The Inner Light Foundation is a non-profit, non-denominational organization engaged in teaching, healing, research and publishing. Formed in 1969, the ILF extends its basic meditation teaching to self-help techniques in the areas of interpersonal communication, health/ wellness, emotional and spiritual growth.
Activities of the ILF include monthly lectures, weekend seminars, and media appearances. The Foundation also sponsors free weekly healing groups open to all, helping individuals find their own answers from the Teacher within.
   Betty Bethards is the founder of the ILF.

Second Printing: September 1983

Cover Design: Jon Goodchild
Cover illustration: John Newman

Printed in the United States of America

In loving dedication to my
husband Greg Huntington,
without whose sensitivity and love
this book could not have been channeled.

TABLE OF CONTENTS

Introduction

by Cary Elizabeth McCarthy, Ph.D.

The word "sex" brings to mind any number of associations. A feeling of delight, a tinge of the forbidden, a sexual partner, a pornographic film, a Masters and Johnson study, or the women's liberation movement. The idea of sex has been loaded with emotional and legal innuendoes for perhaps thousands of years, and it represents something a little different to each of us. The meaning changes as we grow from infancy to adulthood, and it continues to change throughout our lives.

Today we are beginning to look at man wholistically, eclectically, and are beginning more fully to understand our sexual nature. We are borrowing from both physics and metaphysics, east and west, the old and the new. We are attempting to formulate a new perspective, realizing that every part of our lives is related to every other part, and that we cannot understand ourselves when we are compartmentalized or divided into convenient categories.

Is physical sex something that is apart from our spiritual reality? Do we outgrow our need for sex? Does old age preclude sexual enjoyment? Can we be satisfied with one sexual partner throughout our married lives? Do homosexual relationships represent a pathological or healthy trend? Can we expand our psychic and spiritual awareness through sexual experience? Can we increase our capacity for love and pleasure?

For the last several years psychic Betty Bethards has been addressing herself to questions such as these, teaching men and women of all ages how to tap and direct their natural sexual energy, understand sexual preferences and feelings, improve their interpersonal relationships, and expand their level of consciousness—all at the same time. She has lectured throughout California, Arizona and Hawaii, made media appearances, and counseled thousands of people on how to revitalize faltering relationships. Her secret of success springs from her psychic ability to tune into individuals as physical, mental and spiritual beings, and to help them integrate the seemingly diverse parts of their lives.

"Sex is beautiful, exhilarating, and helps you stay young in body, mind and spirit," explains Betty. "The sexual energy is your life force, and we have to learn how to direct it both for fulfillment in sexual love and pleasure and in awakening our higher psychic and intuitional abilities. Through understanding this energy you can create a dynamic love relationship that helps you discover who you are as a person, that helps you grow, and provides a stability *within* in these times of accelerating change. But in order to do this," she continues, "you must learn to change your perspective on the true nature of your being, and get in touch with the inner self. When you realize that you are unlimited, you also begin to discover your infinite potential for joy and love."

About Betty Bethards

Betty is best known as a psychic, spiritual healer, mystic and meditation teacher. Over the last ten years she has become widely recognized through her appearances and her own publications. Thousands have contacted her for psychic readings to help them at crisis points in their lives, and have gained inspiration, insight, and a new sense of direction. Featured in numerous other books and articles, she is called a "superwoman of the supernatural" and one of the top psychic healers in the United States. She has worked with doctors and scientists, exploring and testing her abilities, and in 1969 set up her own Inner Light Foundation for the purpose of teaching meditation and other self-help techniques, publishing, and doing research in expanding human consciousness.

But Betty never intended to start lecturing on sex.

"Believe me, it wasn't my idea," she laughs. "I was raised a fundamentalist Baptist, later turned Methodist, and no one even talked about sex when I was growing up. So when my *channel* first told me that I'd be giving lectures on sex, I said, 'No way, baby, not me! I have too many sexual hang-ups of my own.'"

Betty's channel, she explains, is her psychic or intuitional attunement to her inner teachers. These teachers give her information from levels of consciousness that most of us don't ordinarily have access to. She describes her channel as a high frequency or rate of vibration that one learns to "hear" by attuning to finer energies within. Her gift is similar to that so fully developed in the late Edgar Cayce.

During the years she has grown to trust the soundness of the teachings that "come through" her, via this channel, although she always cautions people not to be gullible on any level of reality.

"Take what feels right and chuck the rest," she emphasizes. "Your soul knows what is truth for you. Don't swallow everything you hear, whether your teachers are in or out of the body. Be your own guru!"

When discussing her teachers, she explains: "Cayce's teachers and my teachers are the White Brotherhood. *White* means light or truth, and has nothing to do with race. These are beings who are presently out of the body and more advanced than we are in their understanding and wisdom. They are teachers of love, trying to help us understand more about ourselves, the age we are living in, and how we can avoid mass destruction. You might think of them as mankind's guardians.

"I communicate with these teachers intuitively or psychically. It takes a great deal of concentration to do this, which I probably developed during my years of pro bowling and working jigsaw puzzles.

"My teachers call themselves messengers of God, and they never give me names because they aren't hung-up in the ego dimension. I just ask that they come of God and be teachers of truth and love."

Betty's lecture, "Sex and Psychic Energy," emerged several years ago when she was "channeling" one evening. "I tried to explain to the channel that I just wasn't the person for the job when they told me that this lecture was going to be added to my repertoire. (She had been lecturing on such topics as how she developed psychically, reincarnation and karma, the meaning of death, how to meditate, and self-healing techniques.) I said, 'I'll go fight violence and ignorance and teach meditation, but leave me out of this sex business.'

"But my teachers explained that the misuse of sexual energy is causing much destruction and violence in the world today, and this is what is preventing us from achieving a world of peace. My teachers said that if we ever want to get it together in our country, to make a success of our marriages, to learn how to love one another, to get the economic and political systems on the right track, we've got to understand how to use and properly direct sexual energy.

"We don't have to worry about nuclear destruction as much as the use of our own energies which are inherently far more potent in their destructive and creative properties. Our creative potential is beyond our farthest imaginings, but our destructive potential equals it in the opposite direction. We are living in an age when we can no longer ignore the fact that we are energy beings, responsible for our own evolution and growth into spiritual consciousness. Although we may think we have all the time in the world to get our acts together, these next 25 years are going to determine whether we make it or break it. And *I* believe we're going to make it, but we've got a lot of work to do!

"Well, to make a long story short, I embarked on a great period of learning, guided by my inner teachers. They were right as usual in the importance, urgency, and meaningfulness of their message. And you know, I never realized that sex could be so beautiful, a road to God consciousness."

Betty estimates she reaches about five million people a year through the media and personal appearances. She has always managed to keep going, never missing a scheduled event. Her motivation is a solid commitment to what she is doing.

"It's really God's foundation, not mine," she emphasizes, "and I really enjoy working for Him."

Her life has not been without trauma, however, including two divorces and the death of her eldest son in Viet Nam. Betty is now happily remarried, and shares her mistakes and triumphs as part of learning to apply the teachings to her own life. And she knows that there is no death because of her own out of the body experiences.

"Everything in our lives provides us with positive opportunities for growth," she often reminds her audiences, "if we but look for the lesson in the experience. God is Love, and nothing ever happens to punish us."

When speaking of death she explains that our loved ones "on the other side are more alive than we are. Death is a celebration, a graduation from school. We should rejoice at death, and send those who continue on into the next dimension our love and support for their journey there. In fact, once we realize that there is no death, we really have to stop and ask ourselves: just what are we here for?"

The answer to this question provides the underlying premise for all of Betty's teachings. What *are* we here for? "To learn," she replies, "Nothing more and nothing less. And it is through our interpersonal relationships and working with the sexual energy or life force that we learn the most."

Coming Up

The following chapters give you a composite of Betty's teachings from many lectures, workshops, individual counseling and channeling sessions. They provide not only theory and insight, but tips on how to apply these ideas in your everyday life, eliminate sexual hang-ups, and open yourself to more pleasure and love. Betty offers no crash course guarantees, no overnight solutions. Instead she teaches a new attitude of living and being, rooted in the daily practice of meditation.

In an era when many are prophesying the end of the nuclear marriage and the "tired ethics" of faithfulness to one mate, Betty responds in a seemingly traditional mode. Commitment to our marriages and maintaining a sexually monogamous relationship will allow us to balance our energies and unfold our greatest potential as humankind.

Yet when many of the traditionalists are declaring their outrage at homosexuality and lesbianism, she maintains that as long as there is a commitment in love to one another, the particular sexual genders are not that important.

Abortion? An individual choice, she says. No one can judge what is right for you. Sadomasochism, the latest fad? A misuse of energy which drains your higher creative ability. And what about sex-change operations? Go ahead, explains Betty, but you chose the sex of your body before you ever incarnated, and the lessons you wished to learn in this life-time. Even if you change your sex, the lessons are still the same. Why not keep your gender and save yourself a lot of time and money?

Divorce? Yes, the rate is rising, but many people who get divorced were never married in the first place. There are very few real marriages, heart-to-heart unions, in the eyes of God.

Living together minus the marriage ceremony? A piece of paper doesn't determine one's state of marriage, she says, only the individuals' commitment to grow in love with one another.

You may discover paradoxes as you go along, the orthodox and the unorthodox. But catch the spirit of her teachings and you will find a message of evolving consciousness, an uplifting and provocative image of mankind today and tomorrow.

Beginning to realize our sexual potential means unfolding our psychic and love potential as well.

Betty Bethards

Chapter 1

Sex, Psychic Energy and You

Understanding Energy

Sexual energy, psychic energy, nervous energy, kundalini, holy spirit, life force—all are terms for the same basic life stuff. They are one life energy, and how we use and experience energy determines how we label it.

This kundalini or life force is housed in all of us as a sleeping serpent at the base of the spine. This is our infinite reservoir of spiritual energy, and when we begin to direct it into higher energy centers of our body we expand our consciousness and begin to walk the path to enlightenment.

We are energy beings, systems of interpenetrating energy fields. We experience ourselves as male and female in bodies, but this is a very limited perception of who and what we really are.

Energy Centers

There are seven basic energy centers in man, called *chakras* from the yogic tradition. The word chakra comes from the Sanskrit term meaning *wheel.* Clairvoyants who perceive these finer energy dimensions of the human system see each chakra as a spinning wheel of energy. Although this has been part of the Hindu tradition for centuries, only recently have we in the West become more fully acquainted with it. We are beginning to realize, for example, that acupuncture and mastery in the martial arts are built around an understanding of the power and flow of these forces within.

Chakras correspond roughly as the etheric dimensions of our endocrine glands. The soul, or etheric body, is connected to the physical body through these centers.

The chakras provide us with the key to understanding ourselves as expanded beings, and the so-called sexual energy is just one of the many manifestations of the force activating these centers—and a very mild one to boot.

The centers are located at the base of the spine, in the sexual organs, the solar plexus, the heart, the throat, between the eyebrows, and the crown of the head. There are many focal points of energy within the human system, but these are the major ones.

Our goal in human evolution is to be fully aware and functioning in and through all these chakras so that we are in perfect harmony and balance, and have awakened our potential as transcendent beings. When our masculine and feminine aspects are balanced, and all our centers are opened and stepped up to a high rate of vibration, we are attuned to the natural, rhythmic flow of life. We are happy and healthy, and know that we are grounded in love and that we are at one with God and all people. Unfortunately, most of us are functioning out of our lower centers only.

Each chakra represents a way of being in the world, a way of perceiving reality. To awaken all the centers we must learn to release the kundalini at the base of the spine, and direct it up the spine and out the crown. If the kundalini gets stuck in any one chakra, we have a lopsided view of reality. This is our biggest problem today—most people are stuck in the second or sexual chakra and are out of perspective.

The *root chakra* at the base of the spine represents minimum existence. Here the person is concerned with sheer

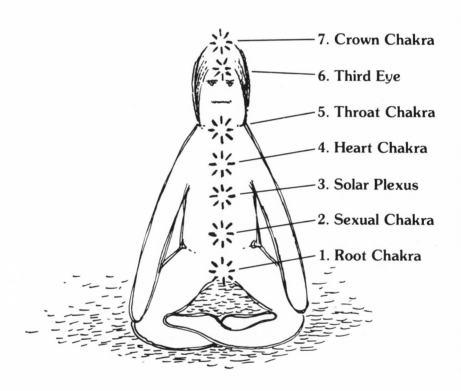

Illustration 1. Major Energy Centers (Chakras) in Man.

survival, brute force, and fear for one's safety. The person is hanging onto life.

If one is operating primarily out of the *second chakra,* he sees other people as sexual objects, things to have, to possess, to exploit. The mind is filled with lust and greed. People are seen as separate from one another. If energy is suppressed or thwarted in this center, violence results. In fact, my channel repeatedly has emphasized that all violence comes from suppressed or misdirected sexual energy. Rape, child beating and child molesting all result from suppressed sexual energy. We must learn not to suppress in any chakra, especially not this one. If people would learn to masturbate rather than hitting their kids or each other, taking their frustration out on everyone around them, they'd get along much better. But masturbation has been seen as a taboo for so long that this simple and easy way to release tension has not been used very often as an alternative to frustration. There is nothing wrong with masturbation, and that energy should not be allowed to build up and come out as destructive behavior. Of course, if you're meditating regularly you are constantly directing this life force throughout your body, and this suppression does not occur. Masturbation is rarely necessary.

The *third chakra* in the solar plexus region focuses on individual power and ego gratification. Self-fulfillment is seen in terms of how powerful and influential an individual can be. This is the center where all the worriers get blasted with fears and insecurities, anything that threatens the ego. Suppression here results in stomach ulcers and other digestive disorders.

There is a close interrelationship among survival, sex and power. These lower three centers view others as apart from ourselves. But realize that none of the centers is "bad"—in fact, all are vital. It is important to be concerned with basic survival while on the earth plane, maintain a sexual orientation and have a sense of ego or personal identification. But these should be balanced and expanded through the awareness that the higher four creative or God centers open up for us.

The fourth center, the *heart chakra,* is the first one in which the genuine unity of love is experienced. It represents the Christ or God within man. And it doesn't matter what religion you may or may not happen to believe in. This Love Spirit is within all of us, call it what you like. When this chakra is closed or walled off we cannot truly feel or love. When the heart center is opened we experience ourselves as part of all life, no longer in competition with others because we are at one with others. Love is the force that abolishes fear, aggression and self-seeking.

If we have sexual unions without the heart chakra being opened, it is second chakra sex only. The same release of tension occurs as in masturbation, and it leaves us drained rather than mellow and full. Unfortunately, many marriage partners are operating out of their second chakras and are experiencing mutual masturbation rather than a love fulfillment. Without the heart chakra open there is always a sense of dissatisfaction. We have the feeling that something is missing, and that maybe we can find it with another partner, or another and another. But what we seek is within ourselves. We will never feel truly united, merged, or at one with ourselves and our partner until we tune into the energy of love. Then when we make love our energies are blended with one another. It is a spiritual union as well as a physical and mental one. To have a sense of completion we must account for the total man: physical, mental and spiritual.

The fifth center, the *throat chakra,* is associated with higher creativity and clairaudience. When we begin to function more fully from this center we tune into levels of inspiration and insight that reach beyond time and space. A writer, a musician or artist would be trying to pull the energy into his higher centers in order to perceive and create ideals of beauty and harmony. The great works of art come from these higher levels of intuition, and this is why there are so few great artists. Most of them are operating from the lower three chakras, and their work hasn't yet taken on the quality of the eternal. If you see a painting and it reflects a violent feeling in you, realize that the person who created it was coming from his second chakra.

The sixth center, located between the eyebrows, is also known as the *third eye.* It is associated with the opening of true spiritual knowledge and psychic potential. Here we no longer perceive the world as filled with paradoxes, but we see with the one eye of truth. Energy emitted as a beam of light from this center is more powerful than a laser, and has tremendous healing properties.

The seventh center, the *crown chakra,* represents union with the God-head, at-oneness with the universe, and is the center of total enlightenment. After you have been meditating for awhile the last two centers merge into one.

All these chakras are open in degrees, but we tend to operate out of some more than others. Very few persons on the earth plane today consistently function from their higher centers, opened and balanced with the lower ones, really in touch with the all pervasive energy that unites mankind.

What It's All About

In order to understand what sex is all about we have to know something about our own energy and how we are experiencing it. Most of us know what it feels like to be turned on sexually: there's a powerful current or sense of desire that can almost overwhelm us. It is something we can't rationalize. We have to experience it. But when we are experiencing it, there's no mistake that it's a real feeling. And that's just in your second center! Imagine what you'd feel if this energy intensity were moving throughout all your centers at the same time!

You as Male-Female

Each one of us is both male and female, knowledge and intuition, yin and yang. We choose to be one sex or the other in order to help us balance the masculine and feminine, the strength and sensitivity, within us. We are bisexual beings. What culture we are living in, what attributes are ascribed to a particular sexual role, also plays a large part in our choice. Masculine and feminine actually cannot be separated when viewed from a perspective of total man; however, we have learned to associate the masculine with assertiveness and strength, and the feminine with passiveness and sensitivity.

Masculine and feminine also are linked with the right and left sides of the brain. The right is associated with intuition and interdimensional awareness; the left with intellect, reason, and time or linear awareness. The left helps us stay grounded and function in our world, but the right is our door to God consciousness. We need to be complete in both our thinking and feeling, knowledge and perception. They are complements, not opposites. Our real awareness results from the dynamic blending of the two, plus the opening and balancing of all the major energy centers of the body.

This concept of being both male and female goes back thousands of years, in mythology, astrology, alchemy, and many other esoteric disciplines. The word "sex" itself means "separate", and we have perceived ourselves as separated from one another. The goal of humankind's evolution is to reunite the male and female, symbolized in an act of sexual intercourse. But the real synthesis occurs between the male and female aspects of the individual self. It is only when this perfect blending *within* occurs that one feels whole, at one with himself, others, and the universe.

Thus sex is much more than passion or the animal instinct to procreate. It is a drive within each of us, the attraction of the male and female aspects within the self, to reunite. The force that propels us to become whole *from within* is the most powerful expression of energy in the universe, and this is the energy of Love. We must learn to love ourselves, to unite this energy *within*, before we are truly free to love others.

Uniting Inner Polarities

Part of the women's liberation movement is attempting to say that women can think, feel and experience as men, and vice versa. In many ways this and other movements, such as the lesbian and gay liberation, are doing us a great service by pointing out that barriers between the sexes are in most cases artificial. This is a period of time, however, when we must realize that manifesting our individuality and our sexuality, our proclamation for individual rights, goes far beyond race, economic group, physical sex, gay bars, swinging, and "coming out." This whole masculine-feminine thing must be viewed in terms of growing into higher consciousness and learning to love the polarities within ourselves as well as learning to love other people. We are not meant to oppose one another. We must transcend a limited consciousness of who we are.

The whole key to do this, of course, is meditation. Meditation combined with building sexual attunement to your partner opens you to levels of love within yourself that most of us have only had glimpses of.

Meditation and Tantra

The best way to raise the energy into the higher centers is through meditation. And working together, from the sexual-love union, one can use a meditative or tantra technique to bring the sexual energy up the spine and awaken both partners to a spiritual merger. In fact, the closest thing we can experience to the God consciousness on the earth plane is the merger at the moment of orgasm.

Mystics of all great religious traditions describe their moments of ecstasy with the same words used to describe the true sexual blending and oneness: at one with God, loss of ego boundaries, merging with the infinite, a sense of the ineffable, total joy and peace, feeling a part of all life. When two persons joined in the love bond properly channel this energy between them, they will experience an out of the body merger together with the God-force. They are reborn, revitalized.

Yet few religious teachers have been willing to admit that the use of the sexual union to achieve God-consciousness is valid and important to mankind's evolution. The tantra or sexual yoga practices often receive raised eyebrow evaluations or are completely dismissed. The sexual drive was and still is seen as man's lower nature, to be avoided at all costs. Because of these and many other misinterpretations sex and the sexual act have been labeled sinful, dirty, or unclean. Nothing could be further from the truth. Any act done in love is of God. Any act done without love is done in ignorance, whether having sexual intercourse or planting a garden. The whole idea of the sexual union is to enable man to re-experience his oneness with God through joining in love with another.

Particularly in the culture we are living in, which largely focuses on the exploitation of sex, it is all the more important that we see sex for its true purpose, and transmute this energy that is already activated by the media into a process for evolving into higher consciousness.

Reincarnation, and Why We're Here in the First Place

Earlier I mentioned that you choose your sex. This goes along with my acceptance of reincarnation, and the idea that nothing in life is a coincidence. If you don't believe in reincarnation, fine. When my channel first started telling me about it, I didn't believe it either. I fought it for a long time coming from a fundamentalist Christian tradition. But finally it began to make more and more sense. It began to explain to me why some people are born blind and some in perfect health, some rich and some poor, and some die in infancy and others live to a ripe old age.

In a nutshell, reincarnation is the idea that we have not one but many lives on this planet. We have so much to learn about ourselves and the universe that we couldn't possibly learn it all in one brief life span. So we keep coming back. Each time we choose a particular situation that we feel will help us learn the most. After we have balanced our energies, and learned all that we can from the earth plane, we then may move into a higher plane of learning and growth. There are seven planes, and seven within each seven. And when we grasp the reincarnation idea we realize that there is no such thing as death.

My channel explains death and the reincarnation process this way:

"Death is the inevitable transition which every soul who incarnates into the physical body must make. It is nothing more than leaving the physical vehicle behind in preparation for higher teaching which all souls undergo. Each soul will incarnate in his own time and in his own way in the vehicle which will give him the best opportunity to achieve growth in that incarnation.

"As he goes through the life experiences, he works to achieve within himself the spiritual, mental and physical balance which is necessary to advance to a higher plane at the time of so-called death. Death is a freer state which does not limit the soul to time and place as you know it. It enables him to see more clearly the things he has gained during his last incarnation on the earth plane.

"Death is a change in the rate of vibration. As you go to sleep at night, and your consciousness leaves the physical body, you are experiencing the same thing as death. See yourself in the dream state. What do you look like there? The body that is you in the dream state is your etheric body, the same you will have at death.

"The only difference between the death state and the dream state is that the silver cord, which is much like an umbilical cord connecting the soul with the body, is severed in death. This cord allows the spirit to travel in the realms and planes beyond the physical at night, and to receive higher teachings. In the state of so-called death, the energy—your spirit—leaves the body and does not return."

The channel says that physical death is like a graduation, and that what we distinguish as *life* and *death* are "different rates of vibration in a continual process of growth and unfoldment. The Life Energy, or God, underlies all experiences of 'life' and 'death' and is the Changeless. As you begin to understand the Energy behind all appearances, all cycles and stages of growth, all transitions, you begin to identify with the Process rather than its manifestations. You begin to identify with the eternal nature of your being, rather than the stages you are going through."

It is important to know that you will never incarnate into anything less than a perfect body unless you deliberately choose it. For example, anyone who has an impairment of the physical senses is working on developing the corresponding higher psychic sense.

My teachers also have said that we incarnate again only as people, that we do not come back as animals as some groups believe. We go through many lifetimes, playing many different roles and parts, both male and female, to learn who and what we are. We are learning about energy, mind, the laws of the universe, and usually very slowly gaining an awareness of the true God-self within us. This is the whole purpose of each incarnation—to learn more about how to love and experience our unity with all life. And there's no copping out. If we don't learn something in one life, it will be waiting for us again in the next.

Earth, then, is like a school. We must develop our abilities to the fullest. When we cross over at death, the first thing our teachers will ask us is: "Did you develop your potentials?" They could care less about who we've been sleeping with.

When we are in that timeless limbo on the other side before we reincarnate, we are very wise in our choosing in what will help us grow and learn the most. We determine the lessons we want and what sex will be the most helpful. You see, you choose your sex (the soul has no sex), your place and date of birth, parents, environment, economic conditions, and race. Nothing is by chance.

When you choose your parents, you walk with them for three years before you actually are born into the world. There is really no such thing as adoption, because you walk with the parents who will be raising you. Your physical mother would be one you had no karma with. By the same token, there is no such thing as abortion. The entity would know whether you would decide to abort the fetus, so you wouldn't be destroying a soul who had planned to come into the world. (The entity does not stay in the developing fetus much of the time, anyway, but goes in and out of the body. When the child kicks or you feel it moving inside you, the entity is "in." Otherwise, it doesn't want to restrict itself to that limited environment.) You are the only judge of whether abortion is right or wrong for you. If you have karma with a particular soul or have agreed before you incarnated to use your body as a vehicle for its entrance to the earth plane, then you intuitively would feel that abortion for you would be wrong. Otherwise, the fact that you got pregnant may simply be a learning experience for you to be more careful, or to work through the relationship with your partner, or numerous other things. But feeling guilt over a necessary abortion serves no purpose and is needless.

Also, in the light of the fact that we do choose our sex, it seems rather useless to go through all the expense and discomfort of sex change operations. Even if a person changes the physical sex of the body, the lessons one initially chose before incarnating remain the same. In fact, after the sex change they may seem even more difficult, because in the soul's initial wisdom it knew what it was doing to select one sex over the other.

If there is going to be a divorce in your family, you know that. If your parents are liberals or fundamentalists, you know that. You know the attitudes your parents have toward sex, and the kind of upbringing you will have. If you are coming into a family of alcoholics, you are already aware of it. You know ahead of time what's going to happen over the next 20-28 years, and you have carefully planned your time of incarnation with other people who will help you work through some karma.

If you are asking why you might choose to incarnate into a seemingly negative environment, it is probably because you dished out the same behavior to others in a previous lifetime and you want to learn why not to do it. And if you are prejudiced in this lifetime against a particular race or economic group, you will probably choose to be born into that very situation next life to help you learn acceptance and sensitivity.

But remember you are always a free agent, and may choose to respond to any situation in a positive or negative way. It is your own attitude, even as a child, that determines your reality.

When you look into the eyes of a baby during its first year of life, you are looking into the eyes of a soul that is in touch with far more than you are. That first year of life the soul can choose not to stay if it thinks, "Gee, I really bit off more than I can chew." Maybe the soul isn't happy in the sex it has chosen, or decides it would rather have different parents, or whatever. If so, it's free to leave. This is the reason for the so-called unknown crib deaths. There is nothing wrong with the child. He just decided to leave. From one to three years old, however, we have to have permission to leave from what I call our "board of directors," our teachers on the other side. As long as the soft spot is open in the crown, we can go. But once the crown is closed, we're stuck, and we have to walk through all the tests we've set up for ourselves.

We all have a team walking with us. If you think you're walking through life alone, forget it. You should be so lucky. You always have a team of teachers with you who are setting you up for all your lessons, helping you learn things you came back to learn, hearing your every thought and word, and watching your every action. And we all have a guardian angel. Catholics have known they are supposed to have one, but us protestants and Jews and other religious groups didn't know they were around. Your guardian angel never leaves your side, and keeps what is called your *book of life*. At the end of each lifetime you get to review it, and see exactly where you've blown it or gotten it together, and what you're going to need to work on the next time around.

Why is reincarnation so important? It puts the choices and responsibility solely on the individual's shoulders. It goes hand in hand with the law of karma: as you sow, you reap. There is no copping out, no more blaming your parents, friends, associates, or "the breaks" for messing up your head. When you incarnate you know where you have weaknesses. You know where you've got to get in and work on building your strengths. You're going to be constantly confronting these things. So everything that you set up for yourself has a lesson. Until you see what it is you'll keep making the same mistakes over and over. It's really very simple and clear. As soon as we learn what a particular kind of experience or attitude is teaching us, we never have to go through it or experience it again.

Reincarnation as a theory has gained much wider acceptance in the Western world in recent years. Although the idea has been condemned by some as destroying initiative and a degrading outlook, rightly understood it serves as the motivator to learn as quickly as possible and advance toward higher consciousness, knowing that we have to learn it now or later. It motivates us to get in there and learn it now in order to move on to other lessons. There is no such thing as being condemned to a certain lot in life. If we're meditating we can move through several lifetimes in one, and move through the initial lessons we established for ourselves at the outset.

A lot of people are interested in past life readings, but actually I wouldn't give you a nickel for them. You can't prove them. If you are interested in any particular periods in history it means you were probably there. We all want to think we were somebody great. But if we were so great we wouldn't be here now. Somewhere along the way we blew it, and we're back to correct the errors. Not for punishment, though, simply to learn the best course.

Your Physical Body

The physical body is your special earth suit that you have chosen to help you learn how to play a particular role better and to work on developing certain strengths. Its unique characteristics and your physical appearance are unmatched anywhere in the universe. When we begin to realize what magnificent vehicles our bodies are to help us learn in this realm, we begin to appreciate them much more. But the body is a mask, a facade. It's what's inside that is important.

Our bodies are made in the image of God, and they are beautiful. The body is not something to feel ashamed of or reject in any way. It doesn't matter what your build is, because the vibrations you're sending out are going to turn people on, not whether you're fat, skinny or in between. What's going to draw people and keep people in your life is what you're radiating from within yourself. This determines whether people feel comfortable with you or back away.

It also may help to remember that just as each of us has been both male and female in bodies in past lives, we have also been both homosexual and heterosexual. Homosexuality is simply a transitional time for the soul. The entity is changing sexes, and usually it takes two incarnations to complete this. For example, if I'd been a woman for several incarnations, and then incarnated into a man's body, I would still feel like a woman inside and may be uncomfortable with my newly acquired masculine body. But as we develop both masculine and feminine aspects of ourselves, we become comfortable with whatever body we may happen to have chosen, and we begin to unite the polarities within us as one powerful energy.

Age of Great Importance

My channel repeatedly has stressed the importance of understanding sexual energy. They have said the fire that could destroy the world, referred to in the Bible and other religious scriptures, is the kundalini fire energy or life force within man, stuck in his second chakra. In other words, it is the misdirection of energy within ourselves that will determine whether we survive as a planet or wind up in a self-destruct pattern. They explain:

"Sexual energy is a lower aspect of the creative force, or God force. When activity is based solely on the lower chakras, particularly the second chakra, the energy of the entire planet resonates at a lower vibration and produces lower animal behavior and environmental disaster. Violence, hatred, greed and selfishness are all lower energy emotions.

"There is only one energy, and it may be used to create or destroy. If one uses it primarily for self-pleasure or sexual gratification, then he is using only the lowest portion and at the same time preventing the higher centers within himself from being replenished, regenerated and developed. The energy is in all of you and links you all as one. This is why what harms one harms all; what helps one helps all.

"We are not denying the expression of sexual love, for this has its importance in your growth, in your polarity with one another, and when properly channeled in the development of higher consciousness. If mankind is to awaken his highest potential and avoid disaster, he must not ignore the sexual force. He must consciously direct this energy up the spine into the higher centers or chakras and feed them so they will in time manifest man's greatest potential."

We really are living in an exciting age, with a tremendous responsibility for determining our own fate. Violence has never worked in the past, and it will never work in the future. The only way we can help the human experiment result in a happy ending is working together in love, that is, through awakening our higher centers.

Ever since the comet Kohoutek entered the earth sphere we've been getting bombarded with extra doses of energy. A lot of people thought the comet was a flop, but it wasn't. Now every full moon brings more and more energy to the earth plane. Much violence and crime occur during the full moon because people just don't know how to handle the increased energy they are feeling. But we've got to get control of this energy, and properly direct it through our systems, if we're going to get our trip together. It's a great time to get our spiritual natures awakened because we have so much energy to work with.

Awakening energy in one level can enhance all other levels, if we know what we're doing. We should strive for balance, being free and open from the tip of our spines to the crown of our heads.

When we really begin to experience ourselves and our partners using both higher and lower centers, we find fulfillment. Boredom leaves us forever, and life truly becomes a process of learning, growing and loving. Beginning to realize our sexual potential means unfolding our psychic and love potential as well. We can direct this energy into higher centers of creativity and begin to realize ourselves as infinite beings.

Chapter 2

Cycles, The Times of Your Life

There are several major cycles in our lives which help govern our growth and understanding. First, two of the most important times during a person's incarnation are at puberty and menopause. The kundalini or life force kicks up naturally at these periods giving us increased energy for transitioning into new stages of development. But these major cyclic changes are rarely if ever understood from a spiritual point of view.

Also, every seven years we go through major cycles of change, completing the old and moving into the new. Every seven years not only has every cell in our bodies been replaced, but we have replaced old attitudes and ideas with new ones.

And besides these cycles, we are subject to yearly growth and renewal periods. We move through points in our own lives corresponding to the seasons of nature: planting of seeds, growing, harvesting and assimilating.

All of these cycles are for revitalizing and regeneration, not for becoming devitalized and aged. Old age, as I will discuss later on, is primarily a matter of programming which we can change.

Puberty

When the kundalini energy is activated naturally at puberty, it is bringing the entity into the realization that he or she is a particular physical vibration. The whole body chemistry is coming into alignment. The energy is transforming the body into the vehicle that will help one learn a great deal about himself throughout this lifetime.

The beginning of the girl's menstrual cycle and the boy's first wet dream should be times of celebration. But how often are girls told that they have now been given "the curse," which suggests that something dirty has happened to their bodies. And often the first wet dream terribly frightens a boy, and his only understanding of it is gained through snickering and whispering with other boys about sexual fantasies.

Parents, ideally both the father and the mother, should sit down with the son or daughter and openly discuss the meaning of the changes in the body, and the meaning of the sexual fantasies that emerge in the consciousness of both boys and girls. In this way young people can learn more about the unfolding of their own sexual natures and not feel guilty or embarrassed about images that are appearing in their dreams.

Parents should reflect a spirit of enthusiasm and delight in the development of the child into adulthood. Also, parents should discuss masturbation with their children, and how they can learn to experience their bodies and discover what feels good and turns them on. Children should be told the purpose of masturbation, which is to help them learn more about themselves and to release energy, but at the same time should be given an understanding of what this energy really is. If they understand that the sexual energy they are feeling is the same as their life force, and that they can direct it through the many different energy centers, they will be very interested in increasing their own mental and intuitional development much more so than focusing on an over-indulgence in masturbation.

If children are told what to expect at different stages of sexual excitement, the true meaning of having a sexual relationship with someone else, how to prevent pregnancy, how to prevent venereal disease, how to use the energy in creative activities, a very healthy sexual attitude can be developed in the mind of the child. Openly presenting this information does not mean that children will engage in rampant sexual activities. It does not result in more sex, but results in wiser sex. Those who are going to experiment anyway will save themselves a lot of heartache. But sex, when put in its proper perspective as one of many avenues to explore in developing the whole mind-body-spirit organism, no longer becomes a primary focus in the teenager's mind. If sex is no longer a mystery, something considered bad or taboo, then there is no need to exploit it. Teens with an adequate understanding and guiltless orientation toward sex take much more responsibility and are more disciplined in their behavior than those teens who feel they are subjected to the arbitrary rules and attitudes of parents.

My teachers have emphasized that they are not trying to turn people on to sex, or to encourage free love. What they are pointing out is the need for open communication about the sexual energy, and the importance of helping children grow up with a healthy attitude that will enable them to build happy and creative lives. Teenagers' lack of preparation and guidance in understanding their own sexual natures is the primary cause for rebellion, violence, and much of the friction that exists between parent and child in the home.

I have been asked by some people at lectures if, in the name of education, the child should be allowed to observe the parents having sexual intercourse. This, I feel, is something that is quite private between two people, and the child would not understand the energy or the experience. It could even be damaging to the child's orientation toward his own body. Seeing films or pictures of sexual intercourse is sufficient. However, if the child accidentally walks in on the parents in the act of love making, the parents should maintain the attitude that everything is fine, and not put out guilty, angry or embarrassed vibes to the child. The parents should discontinue their love making, and gently explain that this is a way of touching and feeling and sharing together that husbands and wives enjoy. Often a child's first reaction is one of fear or horror if he suddenly sees his parents making love, depending on his upbringing. Care should be taken in helping him feel good about his experience and to understand that this behavior was nothing unusual or unloving.

Especially during this period when children begin a self-exploration through masturbation they tend to form what might be misinterpreted as homosexual relationships. Girls may masturbate with and explore other girls, and boys with boys. But these are not homosexual alliances, but result from a simple curiosity to learn about how their bodies respond. Initially they may be more comfortable with a member of their same sex. If parents find their sons or daughters masturbating with friends of the same sex, they should be very careful not to put a "you're a homosexual" trip on them. This behavior represents part of their normal emotional development, and unfolds naturally into an interest in heterosexual relationships.

Young teens begin to be actively interested in forming relationships with members of the opposite sex as the energy of puberty builds momentum. They learn to experience and appreciate many different personality types, and through these relationships they develop their own personalities, learning to understand themselves better.

Young people in their early teens usually have no real understanding of the meaning of the sexual energy, however, and sexual intercourse as a way of experimentation can lead the soul into much unnecessary heartbreak and negative programming that it may take years to change. It is much better to use the energy in developing talents and abilities than forming a lot of sexual alliances.

In the late teens or early twenties, however, premarital sex sometimes can be beneficial, depending on the maturity of the individuals. Far too many people marry without any sexual experience and find they are totally ignorant of the roles to play, how to feel, give and receive. Often this lack of experience is destructive to the marriage. I first married at seventeen and idealistically thought that this would last forever. But I'd had no dating experience, and had no idea what my needs were or what my partner's needs were. And I didn't know how to communicate.

If a person has had some sexual experience, becoming aware of the intensity and blending of the male-female energies, and has begun to learn how to communicate his feelings to another, he often can contribute to a more meaningful marriage relationship. My channel has said that there is no karma associated with pre-marital sex (and often there is no karma associated with what we call adultery, because the individuals involved aren't really married in the eyes of God).

The energy at puberty must be released, and it must be used. It cannot be suppressed in the body. For this reason many children active in sports, music, dancing or some other physical activity have fewer problems and are less drawn to masturbation. The young person involved in some form of creative activity will find that the age of puberty will heighten his gifts. He will be far more creative from that moment on than he ever was during the childhood years.

The energy at puberty is as strong as it is at menopause. But we seldom think of it that way. Puberty is a traumatic time simply because we have not been told what's happening. The sexual change within us is not openly discussed and welcomed, and we don't know how to handle the energy. If we have learned to meditate as children, we have already been balancing and heightening the energy within us. Our emotional natures have become more stabilized and puberty is a harmonious time of channeling these increased energies into creative activities and exploring the meaning of interpersonal relationships. It should be a time when we are laying the groundwork for forming a lasting relationship with a life partner.

Menopause

The next time the kundalini energy naturally comes up is at menopause. This happens for men as well as for women. This is another chance to feel and use the life or sexual energy to renew your body, mind and spirit. But most of us don't realize it is a time for renewal. We never hear that. Instead, we think that menopause marks our time for going over the hill. Now we are getting old. What a terribly distorted view of this phase of our lives!

Menopause involves a hormonal change for both men and women. We are used to associating hormones and youth with the physical cycles of our bodies. This is a lower level of functioning. We can transmute the energy at menopause, and our spiritual or higher centers will begin providing the hormones and vigor we need to maintain strength, youth and agility. In other words, our lower three centers aren't going to work effectively for us anymore all by themselves, and it's time to get the higher creative centers in working order. It doesn't mean no sex—it means better sex. The irony of it is if we continue to identify ourselves with second chakra functioning, we program ourselves as getting older and we lose a lot of our ability to feel and experience pleasure. But if we pull the energy up into our creative or God centers, it brings us into a deeper understanding of love. We *enhance* the sexual function and add a deeper dimension to its expression.

Many women say they get hot flashes and feel like they are going crazy. Both women and men get turned on to new and often younger partners. First of all, if you've been meditating for awhile you know that hot flashes aren't any big deal. When you activate the kundalini energy in meditation you feel this heat, tingling, or energy sensation all over your body. In fact, this is what you want to do, sensitize yourself to higher and stronger energy vibrations. You are learning to process more and more energy through your system.

The renewed interest in sexual turn ons is because the energy that's kicking up is hitting the second chakra and staying there. Thus you are having feelings of sexual desire. Again, when a person first starts meditating he may get turned on as he naturally brings the energy up the spine. I've talked with a number of people in their sixties and seventies who suddenly found themselves fantasizing after six months to a year of meditation. The key is to realize what's happening, and to continue to pull the energy up into your higher centers.

The feeling of insanity results when we haven't been conditioning our nervous systems and brains to handle that energy like we should have been. For example, after a particularly intense meditation period one night I felt terribly dizzy and sort of blown out. My head was spinning. I asked my channel what the problem was, and they said in a somewhat unflattering manner, "Your brain isn't used to all that energy." Thanks a lot. Well, the feeling of losing one's mind at menopause is no different. Beginning to balance and control the increased energy will correct the discomfort.

If you're in a partnership or marriage relationship at the time of menopause this is a great opportunity to get your relationship going in more fulfilling directions. When two people go through this experience at the same time and understand what an opportunity it is, they can create something very beautiful together. The love bond grows much stronger, and through balancing their energies together they receive renewed strength, power, and vigor. Menopause represents a crisis only because of lack of understanding. It should be a time marking the discovery of new and exciting dimensions of ourselves, continuing to maximize the growth process in this incarnation.

When the energy kicks up and hits the second chakra,

sometimes people say they are entering their second child-hood. This really should be a time of entering renewed youth-fulness and revamping the childlike spirit within us. And again, this is why it is so important to understand the spiritual dimensions of what's happening so we don't just have a few sexual flings and then settle back down into our old ruts.

After Menopause and the Later Years

A person's sex life should be as active at 100 as it is at 40. We have outdated ideas about aging and our right to sexual enjoyment, which are programmed in at a very early age and reinforced throughout our lives. Too few people understand what God meant when He said to truly love one another. It means the sexual expression as well as brotherly feeling and tenderness. If we could get it out of our heads that at a certain point in our lives we are no longer supposed to enjoy sex, we would be in a far healthier state and filled with a lot more God consciousness.

Unfortunately, many of us have never learned how to enjoy pleasuring ourselves. We have put pleasure *after* work, and have learned to feel guilty about the things we indulge our-selves in. We forget that loving and nourishing the God-self is the most important task during our lifetime. Getting to know who we are includes exploring and experiencing our potential for joy and pleasure. Many of us have not achieved sexual freedom, realizing it is our right to enjoy our bodies, to live and love fully. But you can establish this attitude of freedom in your consciousness at any age, even if for years you have considered yourself impotent or uninterested in sex. To do this you must go within through meditation and develop a healthy self-attitude—physically, mentally and spiritually. You must learn to love your body, care about yourself, and know you deserve pleasure and love. You must realize that you can experience genuine love in a one-to-one relationship.

Most of us have a difficult time imagining that our parents have sexual relations. We have a difficult time realizing that elderly people need and enjoy sexual intimacy just as much if not more so than anyone else, that is, until we ourselves are labeled "elderly." Then we realize that the desire for love and sex never stops, unless we program it out of our lives. If the elderly person is healthy and happy he is going to have the same functions and same feelings as one who is much younger in years. Much has to do with the individual's physical, mental and emotional balance, of course.

One of the saddest things done by our society is to separate our older citizens, first by putting them in homes, and second, by separating the men and women from each other in those homes. We completely deny the elderly their sexual natures. This causes low self-esteem and feelings of increased worthlessness. Then age sets in all the more quickly. Touching, loving and caring is never outdated. The orgasm can be even more beautiful in the older years, because hopefully our energies are more centered, our heads more together, and the experience is on a higher level of consciousness. The spirit has no age. We are just going through a cycle with a particular body for a brief period here on the earth.

We need to banish completely from our thinking any ideas that degrade us in later life. For example, the "dirty old man" syndrome says if you enjoy sex and you've passed a certain age, there is supposed to be something wrong with you. And our mental de-sexing of older women is reflected in portraying older females as little old ladies knitting, or taking care of grandchildren, rather than going on moonlight strolls with the men they love.

As we grow older often the fear of death subtly affects us. Fear in any form is a destroyer of our total well-being. We must then learn to recognize death for what it is, that it is nothing more than a rebirth of our same being into a higher energy manifestation. Anything that we fear we need to directly confront, and release it from our consciousness.

There is no reason for people not to respond to sexual

energies and the sex drive right up to the day they leave the earth plane. As long as the life force is flowing up and down the spine a person is capable of having normal sexual relations. It helps, of course, to stay on a diet that keeps the energy up and to meditate. We need not grow old and lose that energy. If we tell ourselves we are aging we will age. If we tell ourselves we will remain young in energy and young at heart, we will function as young people. It's all in the mind.

Programming youthfulness and health actually changes the cells and atoms within the body, so that the aging process will be greatly slowed down, or even reversed. An elderly person can suggest to himself that health, power and life energy is flowing through the body, and through maintaining this image and orientation he can revitalize this energy. Preparation for maintaining a healthy sex life in later years should begin ideally when we are still youths. Then we are building up positive programming as we go along. But it is never too late to begin at any age.

Sex is not detrimental to health in the later years as some might believe. In fact, one who has an active sex life will have fewer heart problems and conditions resulting from suppression and stress. Remember, if we know how to use energy, age should empower, not weaken us.

Seven Year Cycles

In addition to these periods when the kundalini energy is helping us through two major transition points, every seven years we are going through cyclic changes. Every seven year period from birth represents the completion of a cycle, and so chronologically we are hitting points of change at the seventh, fourteenth, twenty-first, and so on, birthdays. Also, relationships go through seven year cycles, whether marriage, business or friendship. If there are disharmonies or problem areas that need to be corrected they will tend to surface about the fifth year, allowing us two years to iron out the rough spots before starting into a new cycle.

Chronological Cycles

The first seven years of our lives are very important. It is here that we get lasting impressions about sex and our own self-worth from our parents' attitudes. Our parents communicate to us both consciously and subconsciously attitudes about our bodies. If we are playing with our genitals and our hands get spanked or diverted to another object of attention, or if our parents make faces or say "dirty" when we defecate, we begin to develop some permanent notions about parts of ourselves as unclean and unacceptable. (Of course, we chose the parents or people who would be raising us, and these early attitudes are something we'll have to unlearn or reprogram later on). It is most important for parents to remember that a child needs to feel good about his body. This is the first identification of "me." The child should be taught that his body is made in the image of God, and that it is beautiful, special. It should be explained that not all bodies look alike, some are bigger, some smaller, but all are fine. Instilling a strong sense of self-worth and physical security with one's body (not comparing the body shape or size adversely with another child) will do much to encourage the child's development and self-expression.

In fact, the whole idea of "sex education" as something apart from one's natural experience of living is misleading. Understanding our bodies and feelings should be treated with as much emphasis as any other aspect of our daily routine. Every effort should be made by the parents to help the child feel natural and relaxed with his total physical being and its functions. Suppressing sexual curiosity or punishment for masturbating can present tremendous adjustment problems later on in life.

Sex play among children is quite normal. Little boys want to see what little girls look like, and vice versa. Children are naturally very curious about sex and should be given up front answers to any question they might ask. If children don't show a natural interest in their sexual natures it is because they have picked up cues from their parents that "this is not something we talk about." It is the adult's embarrassment about sex that really answers our children's questions. We need to work on releasing our own restrictive attitudes that regard sex as something apart from the natural life force and flow of experience.

The importance of planting positive attitudes about the self in these first seven years cannot be overemphasized. Of course, negative attitudes can be changed later on in life, but it takes a great deal of work and awareness. Since none of us has had an ideal sexual upbringing—we have all acquired a few fears, insecurities and restrictions along the way—we must now work to free ourselves from blocks that limit our ability to give and receive love, to feel and experience pleasure and know we deserve it.

It is also during these first seven years that the child is highly intuitive, with the right side of the brain more functional than the left. But then, as he enters school, the next seven tend to emphasize left-brain functions, reason and analytical thinking, and we forget to nourish and develop the intuitive factor. Ideally, we would add the analytic functions which are important to our adjustment on the earth plane in time-space, encouraging at the same time the development of the intuitional life. This sense of the intuition is what will continue to guide the soul throughout life, when things he has learned from books become outdated and virtually useless.

All too often, from 7 to 14, the child has changed his focus from inner awareness to outer reality. We have discouraged individual creativity and the development of the imagination, which is our link to the God-force. How often do we tell a child, "It's *just* your imagination." A child can easily learn to meditate, however, from about five years of age. Then his transition into puberty will be much smoother.

So our first seven years is our transition from infancy into childhood, and establishes our basic orientation about the self. It provides us with a period of actively using and experiencing the imagination and intuition. The next seven years are our transition into young adulthood. Supposedly, the intellectual functions are brought into balance with the intuitive at this time, but because of the educational system this seldom occurs. From 14 to 21 we are completing our transition into adulthood, and balancing out the energy that was so strong during the teen years. From 21 to 28 we are trying our wings as adults, and often establishing our marriages or partnerships. This is the period when we begin to develop our first sense of independence. Often 28 provides a major turning point in the awareness of the individual. He has moved through those first years of doing what others expected, being caught up in the programs of the past, either playing them out or rebelling against them. Finally he begins to catch glimpses of himself as a free agent, and asks, "What do *I* really want?"

For many people the period from 28 to 35 is the time they really begin to discover their individuality. But it can happen at any time, or not at all. These seven year cycles continue, each one bringing opportunities to cast off the old beliefs and ideas that no longer serve us and give birth to the new. Being aware that often we experience a certain amount of confusion during the transition years of cycles (28-29, 35-36, 42-43, 49-50, and so on) helps in preparing ourselves to stay somewhat detached and keep a positive attitude.

Cycles for Partnerships

The cycles for partnerships, businesses or marriages begin when they are first formed, and then continue through the seven year cyclic periods. In the fifth year of a partnership you should determine what you like and don't like, what is going well and what needs improvement. Of course, you should constantly be aware of how the relationship is going, but it is essential to examine it two years before the cycle is up. This is the time when the energy of this particular liaison is building momentum for change. If you do not correct the weaknesses, you will see real problems surface at the seventh year period. And if the relationship is not growth producing, it will most likely break up. Again, this is not for punishment, or to scare us, but to enable us to do the pruning and refining that is necessary to maximize our growth and happiness.

Partnerships and marriages do not have to break up on these cycles, although many do. If you are working together, these are beautiful transition periods into new and more exciting dimensions together. This is what each cycle offers us. But again, we must accept the responsibility to stay tuned in to what we are creating, and be aware of negative programming and limiting beliefs that need changing. Great relationships don't just happen automatically. We have to work to achieve them. We have to put in a lot of time, love and effort. On the other hand, there is no such thing as a static relationship. Everything is constantly in motion. Whether the motion takes a positive or negative direction depends on how we are using the energy. Remember that the purpose of each cycle and each experience is to help us grow. If we are with someone or in some partnership that is not allowing our growth, God will not let us stay in it, but will move us into another situation.

Yearly Cycles

We also move through yearly cycles which help keep us on our toes, and give us more immediate feedback on where we're getting it together and where we're blowing it.

Every spring when the growing season begins for nature it begins for us, too. To help us grow we are given certain lessons to learn, certain tasks to master physically, mentally, emotionally and spiritually. On a higher level of awareness we have chosen these lessons. If we learn them we move on to greater understanding and new lessons. If we don't, then they will be waiting for us again next, year.

From spring to fall the energy is high, and usually things are happening so fast that we hardly have time to evaluate them. But with the beginning of the fall season and the coming of winter, we have time to reflect and assimilate. If we carefully consider what we have mastered and what we left undone, we'll have a pretty good idea of what will be waiting for us again in the spring.

To discover what you're supposed to be working on at any particular time in your life, ask yourself, "What were my lessons last year?" The lessons are as varied as individual need and evolution. For example, you might be learning how to forgive yourself and others, make decisions, overcome fears of rejection and loneliness, be clear on commitments, accept responsibility, develop a healthy self-image, use a dormant talent, develop a positive attitude toward pleasure, learn how to communicate needs and feelings, or how to love the unlovable.

If you can't identify a lesson, or you aren't aware of anything you've been working on, simply recall any experiences over the last year you thought unpleasant or unhappy. They contained a definite lesson. Happy experiences have lessons, too, but we usually see them more easily. When you are in a quiet meditative state, bring to mind the experience and the people involved in it. Then silently ask: What was the positive lesson I was supposed to have learned from this? If you are really open to seeing it, and no longer wish to place the blame for what happens to you on someone else, then you'll get some insight. You might have been learning about how not to do something, or how to love yourself more so that you realize you deserve better relationships. But on some level of your being *you set up* the experience, and it was only to test whether you had gotten rid of a particular program in your head that limits your growth.

Summary

As you go through your yearly cycles, seven year cycles, and kundalini cycles, remember that you create each situation in your life to teach you something quite special. Begin to look for the positive learning experiences in everything you do. You'll find much of the negative comes from putting yourself down. By learning to love yourself you will avoid much of the hassle you usually create. And remember that each cycle is designed to propel you toward greater understanding and renewed vitality. Thus as we move through our total life cycle, we should become more empowered. We continuously should gain greater self-insight and a greater capacity for love and pleasure. Remember that the soul is ageless, and a beautiful spirit radiates through a body of any age and transforms it.

Chapter 3

Interpersonal Relationships:
The Cosmic Set-ups

Interpersonal relationships provide our greatest opportunity for growth on the earth plane. Each relationship shows us something about ourselves. We draw people to us in life who are going to push our buttons, revealing our old inner programming about ourselves and the world we live in. And the only reason we have incarnated at all is to find out what's going on inside and clear out useless or negative beliefs. Our programs, energy level and dominant chakra are the major contributing factors to how we interpret what's going on in our lives. That's why we have an increased responsibility to meditate on a daily basis. Meditation keeps our energy up high enough so that we have the clarity to look at our numbers, and hopefully change them. Otherwise, our energy is so low that we just get caught in reacting to others, going up and down with their moods, and we can't see how we're setting up our experiences.

A fulfilling sexual relationship begins with understanding the dynamics of relating with others. Sexual communication with your partner reflects your total mind set at any given moment. Worry, frustration and blocks that have resulted from a past or present situation affects your ability to give and receive love openly and completely. We should strive to be aware enough in our interpersonal situations to change any negatives that interfere with our ability to love.

Essential Ingredients

No matter what kind of relationship you're presently involved in, or what kind you'd like to be involved in—job, lover, spouse, parent, friend— the first key to success is communication. Whether a spouse or distant relative, we must establish ways of communicating so that both people can express their feelings and needs. We must be able to talk about and improve our interaction with one another.

It is important to establish a method of communication that allows both people to express themselves, explore, and not be dominated or put down. To do this we have to be willing to listen intently to the other person, and repeat back to him what he has expressed so that we both are sure that the right message has been communicated. What you mean to say, what you actually say, and what I hear you say may be three entirely different messages.

Genuine communication begins with genuine respect for the other person as an infinite being, and one who is participating with you in life's learning process. If we are not willing to communicate our thoughts and feelings to others, not willing to say what is hurting us, and not willing to listen in return, then the relationship does not have much chance of making a go of it.

The next element is commitment. Once we are communicating with one another, we must ask, "What is my commitment to the relationship? What am I willing to do? To give? What is the real meaning of the relationship to me and to you?" Unless we understand the level of commitment from both parties involved, the relationship will be unclear. We will be operating on many false assumptions. You need to define where you both stand, the ground rules of operation, and what your limits are. These, of course, are subject to change and expansion as you go along. Also, if your levels of commitment are different, and one person is willing to give a great deal more than the other, then the relationship is being built on shaky grounds. Each person should be mutually concerned for the benefit and well-being of both himself and his partner, committed to working through problems and keeping lines of communication open.

A third often forgotten essential is appreciation. We won't survive very long in a situation if we fell unappreciated. If you think about any relationships you are involved in today which seem unpleasant or unhappy, you'll discover that the appreciation dimension is missing somewhere along the way. Either you don't feel appreciated in some area, or you aren't giving that appreciation to your partner. If you aren't letting your partner know that you appreciate what he's doing, like his good qualities and recognize his specialness as a person, then a great deal of negativity and insecurity are going to build up. A pat on the back and a kind word are easy to give. Often we just forget to take the time to care.

The other essential element is acceptance. We must learn how to accept one another as worthy human beings. We don't have to buy all the trips someone else is running, but we can let him know that we love and care about him just because he is a fellow expression of the God-energy. It's a vibe that we send out that says, "Whatever trips you're running, I accept you. You don't have to try to impress me, because I've already accepted you. I just enjoy experiencing you as a person." As we really begin to communicate this level of acceptance to others—which must be based on our ability to completely accept ourselves, of course—people begin to put down their defenses. Why do I have to be defensive if someone's already accepted me? Then I can relax, and begin to tune in to and enjoy what I am giving and receiving in the relationship. If the acceptance level in a relationship is conditional, or you feel a definite lack of acceptance, you will also feel a high tension level that interferes with genuine loving and caring. The two people will not feel or be at their best. Begin to send out this unconditional acceptance to people, and watch tension levels disappear in both yourself and others. You'll begin to function more freely as a person, and enable others to do so, too.

Self-Love: The Key to Successful Interpersonal Relationships

Success in our interpersonal relationships begins with our ability to love ourselves. If you don't love yourself you can't love anybody else. If you don't love yourself you'll be running so many insecurity and fear numbers that you'll misread the actions and words of those around you. And in order to both give and receive love fully, you have to feel worthy of love from within, both the male and female aspects of yourself. If you have a basic dislike for women, it means that you are rejecting your own femininity. If you have a basic dislike for men, you are uncomfortable with your own masculine nature.

Loving yourself is one of the hardest things in the world to do. Most of us think we *are* loving ourselves, but when we really get down to the basics we don't even know who we are. It's pretty hard to love someone, especially you, if you don't know yourself in the first place.

But how do we begin to love ourselves? Many people say that we can love ourselves only if others love us, and that the problem of the particular age we are living in is alienation. This technological society has separated us from one another. Well, it has really always been a problem. We feel alone and alienated from others at any point in history when we function primarily out of our lower chakras. We run a lot of programs, such as: I am alone. No one loves me. Love has passed me by. I loved once but I'll never love again. Or a favorite one is: If only she loved me, my life would be happy. That's the trick, we think. To get someone *out there* to love me.

The amazing truth is that no one can give you love. It can't come from anyone or anything *out there*. It comes *from within*. You don't have to go out and look for love, you don't

have to hope for it or wish for it. *You generate it yourself.*
When you begin tuning into that infinite reservoir of love and
well-being within you, the God-self within you, then your
universe, your world, unfolds in love. Because that's what you
are. Love is that energy that unites all of us, and when you
begin to create this love from within, you aren't alone
anymore.

You don't have to wonder if people love you, because you
love them and include them in your world. You see, the
problem is not whether we are loved, but whether we are
loving. In the law of mind like attracts like. As you feel love and
become love from within, you automatically attract it to you in
every aspect of your life.

This idea of generating love from within, being and feeling
from within the love we normally seek from without, is one of
the hardest things we have to work with in our everyday
interpersonal relationships. When someone comes up and
lays a negative number on you, your first reaction is usually
defensiveness. We seldom remember to mentally affirm, "I
love myself, and I love you, and I realize what you said is just
your trip. I accept you where you are, but I don't buy your
negativity." We should practice being so centered in our daily
lives that if the world crumbles beneath our feet it doesn't
matter and won't throw us off. We forget that each one of us is
just playing out a role for this particular incarnation, and that
the other person's behavior is reflecting a part of ourselves.
We take things entirely too seriously.

Whenever you feel you're getting uptight with someone,
silently bless the person and mentally repeat something like
this: "Love enables you to be the best that you can be. Love
enables me to be the best that I can be." This helps restore
your sense of balance.

In order to reach out in love to others we have to keep a
clear perspective in our own heads. Again, that is why I push
meditation. You learn who you are, infinite and unlimited.
You learn to love the God-self within, and stabilize your

energy so that you can keep a perspective on what's happening and why in your daily life, how you're setting yourself up in both positive and negative situations.

To love yourself start looking for your good instead of your bad. When we focus on all the things we don't like about ourselves, we simply pour more energy into the negative. Begin focusing on the positive attributes, and give yourself positive suggestions that you are developing traits to counterbalance those you don't like. For example, if you've been telling yourself that you are sarcastic toward others, begin suggesting that you are becoming more loving and sensitive to those around you. If you frequently tell yourself that you are unattractive, suggest to yourself that you are learning to see your true beauty and are manifesting it in your life. God is in you, as well as everybody else. If you forget to love the God-self, the true you within, you're going to have to incarnate again until you learn it. Recognize your errors, but focus on your good. The God part of you needs that energy.

Why we get off the Track

From the time we're little we want to win approval. Everybody wants love. There isn't one of us who doesn't. And we all fear rejection. This is one of our biggest button pushers. So we quickly learn how to win over our parents and get their attention and love, and we learn how to manipulate friends and everybody else to help us get the attention and sense of self-worth we desire. We're constantly playing a game of being what someone else wants us to be. By the time we're in our twenties, and some of us much later on in life than that, we wake up and think, "Now wait a minute. Who am I?" We don't know who we are because we've been so busy being what everyone else wanted us to be, or reacting against what they wanted us to be.

In the first place you have to realize that you could never be what I want, because whatever I want for you I'm really wanting for myself. You could never please me on a full-time basis, because what I want you to be today I may not want you to be tomorrow. I'll be in a different space tomorrow. And if you keep on trying to find out what will really please me, you're just spinning your wheels. You're never going to get it together and you're wearing yourself out. Decide what *you* want to be. You can create anything you like. Then say, "This is who I am. I like myself this way. If you love me, great, and if you don't that's okay, too. But this is who I'm going to be." Dare to be yourself, and don't apologize. And do you know what happens? When you like yourself, other people like you, too.

But be careful not to confuse liking yourself with how many times you "succeed" or "fail." There is really no such thing as failure, only opportunities for learning. The way we get strong is by falling down flat on our face, making mistakes and learning from them. There is no way you can fail in life. You're going to learn from every experience. And you're never too old to learn. The idea that you can't teach an old dog new tricks is a fallacy. As long as you're occupying your physical vehicle there is something for you to learn here, or else you wouldn't be in the body.

Also, don't think you have to be perfect in order to like yourself. Many of us are terribly harsh judges on ourselves. First, if you were perfect you'd mirror so *perfectly* for the rest of us all our frailties that we couldn't stand you. And secondly, if you were perfect there would be no reason for you to incarnate in the first place. Get in and be honest about where you are. Love yourself both for where you are and for what you want to change, and don't be so concerned with what the other guy is thinking about you. It will change tomorrow anyway.

Bodies, Faces, and Loving Yourself

Some people run "I don't love myself" numbers because they don't like their physical appearance. They don't think they are attractive enough, or handsome enough to ever deserve an exhilarating and fulfilling love relationship.

Remember that you chose your own body and you picked the physical appearance that would help you learn the most. A beautiful body can be a detriment as well as an asset. A very beautiful person is tempted in this incarnation to become selfish and self-centered. Many people will choose sexy bodies in order to work on bringing a balance in that area. Or, a beautiful woman may be forced to develop her sense of inner beauty, because she is plagued by fears of becoming old and unacceptable.

Also, it is easy for those who are exceptionally handsome or beautiful to be tempted in their marriage unions to take advantage of and be unfaithful to their mates. This would result, of course, from their mates running programs of "my partner is so handsome that he couldn't possibly be satisfied with someone as plain as I am."

Many entities choose a plain face in order to help them learn to manifest the beauty within them rather than sliding by on the beauty without. You choose bodies, just like everything else, to help overcome weaknesses and build strengths. One incarnation you could be very beautiful and another very physically ugly. But you are always only as beautiful as you feel inside. People are drawn not to your physical features, but to that which shines out from within. It is the inner beauty that determines a lasting union.

But the key is accepting and loving exactly what you are, seeing the Self within that made the decision in the first place.

Loving Yourself and Credentials

There are many people who feel totally unworthy because they don't have a college degree or some other piece of paper that says they have completed this or that. They go through great pains to pretend that they belong to elite groups or have a certain level of education, or they spend a lot of time apologizing for not measuring up to what they assume others expect of them. But what does it matter if you do or don't have a degree, or belong to this or that organization? What does it matter whether you know important people, or are an accomplished name-dropper? The only person you should really be concerned about how well you know is *yourself*. What counts is whether you're learning the lessons you came back to learn in this incarnation, and whether you're working to balance your intellect and intuition.

A person who is a heart chakra or sensitive and intuitive person is going to be far more successful than someone who is locked in the intellect. With the intuition we can move beyond all present knowledge. All you have to do is begin exploring your inner space.

Understanding Criticism

If you know yourself you can handle anything that happens in your daily life. If people criticize you and you're centered, your energies are high and balanced, it won't bother you. If there is truth in the remark then you can thank them for their observation, and you can begin to correct the error. If you feel there is no relevance in the comment to you, then just forget it. You are only a mirror for others to see themselves in. If someone is yelling at you, you can ask "What's really hurting you?" You can help the individual explore what the problem really is, not get caught up in his trip. You can allow him his own space.

But if people are frequently criticizing you it means that you are putting out a vibe that says, "I'm insecure and I'm afraid that you're going to criticize me." If you put out that vibration others are going to follow through with your programming, and probably won't even be aware of what they are doing.

Anything you are afraid of you draw to you. That's why we must work to rid ourselves of fears, meet them face to face, and dismiss them from our lives. If you're afraid of being robbed, someone's going to pick up on that non-verbal program and rip you off. Then you can say, "See, I told you so." But *you* set it up. All your non-verbal thoughts and feelings are like radio waves, and someone picks them up and comes in and treats you the way you're asking to be treated.

When a woman or man comes to me in a counseling situation and says my husband or wife is sleeping around, I immediately ask, "How did you set it up?" If I have a fear that my partner is going to run around on me, my fear will determine how I experience him and how he experiences me. I will be sending out an attitude of "I'm not worthy to be loved completely by you."

A third party never comes into a relationship unless there is a reason. Something is wrong in your thinking and interrelating and this is to help you look at it. It doesn't mean that one is supposed to run off and marry the new person, but it does mean to stop and look at what is not working and get in there and change it. Your guidance or higher teachers will set you up to look at the numbers you're running on yourself and your partner. Usually it's unworthiness, the fear of rejection, or you're playing the mother or father role rather than the man-woman.

The thing to remember is that all criticism, all negative experiences, are positive learning opportunities. And you can't get away from your lessons. Eventually we learn we're responsible for what's happening in our lives.

Five Husbands Later

Another lady came in to see me and said, "I'll never marry again. I've had five husbands and they all treated me the same. They were domineering and inconsiderate." She thought she was safe. She never stopped to ask what insecurity programs she was running to bring the same kind of person into her life each time. But then she went to work for a new boss, and he played out the same role with her again. I suggested that perhaps it was time to examine her thinking.

We've all got to walk through life. We chose it and we can make it a heaven or a hell for ourselves. Every experience and every relationship you're involved in right now is an opportunity for learning. If you insist on seeing a relationship as negative, you'll never understand what the lesson is behind it, and why you set it up in the first place. Start looking for the positive in people and they will show you nothing but their good side. If you look for the negative they won't disappoint you, either. People act differently from person to person, situation to situation, because they are following through on your expectations. Expect good and only good will come back to you.

When Love First Glows

When you first fall in love, stop and look at what you're really feeling for the other person. You've loved many souls through past lives, and this is one of those relationships coming through in this one. You'd never fall in love or marry someone unless you'd been with them before in a past life. So when you feel this attraction, ask yourself, "We love each other, but how? Is it a brother-sister, father-daughter, mother-son, or man-woman?" If you don't have a strong sexual attraction for one another on the man-woman level, you're not going to have a very successful marriage relationship. If it's a father-daughter or mother-son relationship, there will be difficulty in maintaining the sex vibe, and the relationship will limit the growth of both persons due to the parental role one of them is playing. If your sexual relationship is immediately harmonious and you feel a natural attunement to the person, you most likely have been married or lovers before.

If you fall in love with someone the same sex as you are, and you've never considered yourself to be a homosexual, this may really upset you. But you are drawn to the soul of that person, and you have loved him in a past life. You both just happen to be the same sex this time around. You can flow with the relationship and work on strengthening the sexual love bond, or you can decide that this time you will work on developing the friendship vibration with the person, and instead set up a heterosexual relationship that will be equally as fulfilling. But the choice is always yours, and you should go with your intuitive feelings.

Also, you may love or be attracted sexually to a number of people throughout your life, because you've shared many deep loving relationships in your past incarnations. But just because you meet someone who turns you on when you're already in a relationship or married doesn't mean that you have to jump into a new bed. We don't have time in this life to marry everyone we've loved before. So just acknowledge that you love the other person, and pull the energy up to your heart chakra. You will feel a purer love rather than just the sexual turn on. Wait until you're out of the body and you can have a beautiful merger again. But for now, you might tell your newly discovered friend that you've got other lessons to learn in your present lifetime. It is all in understanding that you are trying to build the kind of energy attunement with one person that will lead you to the greatest degree of self-exploration.

When you first fall in love, what you see in the other person is your own potential that you are afraid to bring out. In other words, I see in you something of the beauty of myself that I have not looked at before. The initial experience of falling in love is seeing the positive, the highest projected image of ourselves onto another. We both see this in one another, but we are really looking at our own self-beauty. We feel like we're soaring and filled with a new sense of energy and well-being.

But then, as we are together longer, I also see in you a lot of my own weaknesses and insecurities, because you are mirroring them back to me. In order to maintain the state of beauty or ecstasy, then, we also must look at the limits, the negative programs we have set up in our minds. It is these negative programs that keep us from seeing and feeling this state of ecstasy all the time, with or without someone else around. So we begin to find fault with the other person. We say that love is wearing off, or perhaps that our love has died. All too often this is where the relationship ends because there is great effort required on our parts if we want to maintain that initial state of beauty. We must work to clear our own consciousness, and never be afraid to look inside and see what is really hurting us. We are a lot stronger than we think we are.

Sometimes we choose to put up a big wall so no one can get through to the "real us" to hurt us. That way we'll be safe, we think. But we're miserable behind that wall, and we might as well open up and begin to experience the beauty as well as the pain of self-discovery.

Most people don't really understand why love makes us vulnerable, or open. It's because love, to be fully expressed in and through your being, begins to eliminate all the fears, all the insecurities and all the anxieties that are inconsistent with itself. Love begins to purify your being, begins to open you up to joys that you never before knew. The vulnerability comes from exposing your own limitations that you have set up, looking at and identifying them. Your freedom comes from realizing that you can let them go, and then you are no longer vulnerable.

So when the negative begins to surface in a relationship, and you feel jealous or angry, look at why the other person has triggered this response within you. Learn how to communicate your feelings, because this is what is really teaching you to communicate with yourself. If you make the commitment in that initial period of loving another person, if you understand what is going to be happening with the energy and programs running back and forth, you will realize that love never really goes away, only your immediate perception of it. And you realize that you must begin to free yourself from negativity and restriction if your awareness of love is to be maintained.

The first soaring of energy and thrilling sensations of falling in love are just to get us interested. Falling in love is somewhat like beginning meditation. Often when a person first starts meditating he sees beautiful colors, lights and pictures, and is enamored by this inner world he never before knew existed. And then all of a sudden the pictures stop, and he thinks something isn't working. For a year or more he may just sit there and stare at the backs of his eyelids. His guidance is asking him: "What are you really sitting there for, the movies? the instant thrills? or to build your energy field and balance it so that you can truly learn to love yourself and get your trip together?"

So it is with love. Guidance will ask when the real work begins, "What are you really in this relationship for? An easy thrill? kind words to build your ego? to maintain your illusions? or are you really in it to get to know yourself, to learn how to truly give and receive love with another?"

Your partner is your best mirror. Whenever you become angry or frustrated with the relationship, remember to say, "Thanks for pushing my button. Now I'll have to see what's really hurting me. Thanks for helping me to see a part of myself."

A Word About Incest

Incest is a highly prevalent and little talked about occurrence. It is not accepted in our culture, and is perhaps one of the most destructive forms of interpersonal relationships. (Although, of course, if you have participated in or have been a victim of incest, you can turn the experience into a deeper understanding of human nature and move beyond it.)

Within the family we must learn the meaning of different roles and develop love bonds that we can extend to all people: parent-child, brother-sister, friend-friend. To confuse this love with sex is a disservice, and will result in confusion in the minds of children as to the real nature and meaning of love and sex in human evolution.

If the parent has been married to a child in a past life, or if brothers and sisters have been married before, a sexual attraction may manifest from time to time. If a family member gets drunk or dulls his senses through drugs, he may find himself turned on to one of the children. With the usual conscious control mechanisms out of the way, he will begin to make sexual advances.

Sexual relations are quite common between brothers and sisters, and are not as damaging psychologically as parent-child incest. It depends, of course, on whether one sibling was forced by the other or both were eager to participate. Again, it is the parents' responsibility to teach their sons and daughters about the meaning of sex, and why it is not encouraged within the nuclear family.

We have chosen the roles of parent-child or brother-sister in this life for good reasons: to help us learn new roles and relate to each other in a different way. If we had thought the lover relationship would have been the most conducive to learning, we would not have set ourselves up as members of the same physical family. We must be able to say, "Hey, I feel turned on, but this time around we have chosen different roles to play." Then pull the energy up to your heart chakra.

We should not use our children sexually, or allow another family member to do so. This is an inherent responsibility for all parents, and we must be strong enough and wise enough to correct and eliminate any such abuses.

A Vision on Relationships

On my forty-second birthday I had a special vision. Suddenly I was watching a terribly stormy sea, and there were millions of little boats tossing and turning in the waves. My channel told me that each one of us is a boat on the waves of life. They said, "Look where most of those people are sitting in their boats. They're not at the helm." Most everyone was in the back of the boat, holding on to the sides, going up and down, being bounced and jostled around. "You may take your boat into any port," they continued, "and form relationships to help you understand yourself and life better. What happens most often is that you go into a port, begin a new job, a relationship, or start a new project, and at the first signs of trouble you decide to leave. You drift back into the stormy seas, with nobody there to guide or chart your course. Eventually you drift into another port, stay there only until the going gets rough and once again leave, still out of control and understanding nothing." They showed me that it is our relationships, the ports, through which we build an understanding of ourselves. It is here that we can develop the strength to take control of our own helm by learning what we need and don't need, want and don't want, and what negative programs are limiting our awareness of our true selves. When we do learn to take control, we can stay in any port, in any situation, and be at peace with ourselves, no longer tossed and turned by the vicissitudes of thought and emotions.

The message was simple enough. We aren't taking control of our lives because we are too lazy to do our homework, to commit ourselves to working through our hang-ups. And we take the same hang-ups with us into every situation until we stop long enough to really look at them, work through them, and let them go.

Taking Control

Recently a couple I had counseled four years ago came to see me again. They said, somewhat disappointedly, that their life was the same as it was four years ago, and what did I see in their future? I said, "The same thing as your last four years." They hadn't been meditating, and they had been making no progress at all in changing their thinking patterns. Unless one makes inner progress he cannot expect to make outer progress. They hadn't taken control of their helms, and were still tossing about on that sea of endless storms.

Another lady reported that I'd told her two years ago that she would probably be married by this time. She wasn't, with no prospective men on the horizon. She still had a big block against getting involved with a man because she was afraid of getting hurt. Her energy field was low. "Have you been meditating?" I asked her, knowing that she hadn't been. She shook her head.

We must realize that we are in control of our own destinies. The way to change your experience or relationship is to ask what you really want, and what would be the most fulfilling thing you could do? Then begin to work on building what you want by focusing your thought energies on achieving it.

The imagination is your key to do this. The imagination is reality. What you *think* about yourself and your experiences is what is going to manifest for you in your life. You're getting exactly out of life what you think you deserve, nothing more and nothing less. If you want more out of your relationships you have to change your ideas and attitudes. Picture and feel yourself in an ideal situation. Feel yourself as totally happy, giving and receiving love. Hold this image in your mind. Refuse to accept anything less than what you want for ideal self-growth and unfoldment, and you will attract that very situation into your life. You are unlimited, and can manifest anything through positive thinking and picturing and feeling the situation as if it has already happened in your life. (Never picture anything that would be injurious to others, however, or you will discover it will backfire.)

If you say you've tried that and it doesn't work for you, then you are giving your subconscious mind conflicting messages. Often people have told me that they wanted ideal love relationships. They programmed their thoughts toward manifesting that relationship, but when it came along they didn't feel worthy of it. Inwardly they had not learned to love themselves enough to realize they deserved it, and so they let it slip away. This sense of unworthiness also manifests when a person continuously falls in love with a married or unavailable person. If you aren't really ready to deal with your programs, and don't want to make the commitment yourself to give and receive love, then you'll be attracted to those persons who aren't free to make a complete commitment to you. Once you realize that you deserve a fulltime relationship you'll attract an eligible partner to you.

Learning from Past Relationships

When we leave our physical body at death, we have an immediate flashback of our lifetime. Often we hear people tell of seeing their whole life in an instant right at the point they thought they wouldn't survive, only to pull out of their crisis situation a few moments later. At the time of our transition we see the whole movie of everything we did and didn't do, and we can't cop out and blame the other fellow for anything. We can see exactly where our heads were, and how we set up the situation, all our negative and positive thinking, and we can't get away with anything! But we don't have to wait until death to review our relationships and see where we are making mistakes, and what lessons we are learning. We can learn right now while still in the physical body to let go of the past, forgive everyone who needs forgiveness, including ourselves, and move on to richer and more fulfilling lives.

Make a list of all the people who have been fairly significant in your life. Be sure to include those with whom you had both positive and negative experiences. My list included over 60 people. Your's might have a lot more or less, depending on your background. Beside each person's name, write down the positive lesson that he or she taught you. You may not think you know what the lesson is, but you'll discover that it is fairly easy to identify once you carefully evaluate the meaning of the relationship for you. The lesson may have been how to stand on your own two feet, that positive support ultimately must come from within rather than from without, or how to make decisions. Any past love relationship usually has one major lesson, and perhaps several little ones.

This process of listing all the names and the positive growth lesson beside each one may take you a day or two. But you will be amazed when you finish at how important each one of these people has been in your life. Even some of the ones you thought were insignificant or that hurt you at the time had very important lessons to teach you. This process begins to help us think in positive terms, and to release any destructive thoughts that are binding us to the past. Hovering mentally around a particular relationship wondering why the person did such and such to you doesn't help you learn and move on.

Once the lesson is spotted, recognize it, learn from it, and then release it. No matter what you or anyone else has done or not done, it can be turned into positive self-insight.

Realizing that everyone sets up his or her experiences, however, does not give us a free license to go around doing anything we please to others. When we become more aware, the idea is not to play into another person's negative programs, but to respond with the love he needs to help him look at and rid himself of limiting beliefs.

Chapter 4

Marriage,
The Last Frontier

The Heart-to-Heart Union

"In the eyes of God, there are very few marriages," my channel emphasizes, "for true marriage is a heart-to-heart union, a commitment from each partner to grow with and love the other. The true marriage union enables both persons to advance toward self-understanding and enlightenment at a rapid pace. It is a physical, mental and spiritual bond. Love is shared and experienced by a blending of energies from all the chakras, and it enables both partners to soar to new heights unknown, discovering more about themselves and each other day by day."

It doesn't matter whether or not you have a piece of paper signifying a legalized marriage. If you have the love union between you, you are in effect married.

The true marriage is one of the last frontiers that we haven't even begun to explore. In fact, many people are ready to throw away what they call traditional or nuclear marriage because they say it is too limiting. Swinging and experiencing a lot of different partners is what we need, they argue. There are so many facets of our personalities that we couldn't possibly find fulfillment with just one other person. And here the argument misses the boat entirely. As I've emphasized earlier, we can't find fulfillment with a thousand other persons until we find it within ourselves. We begin to do this by stabilizing our energies and focusing on self-growth with one other person, qualitatively expanding our understanding of life, love, and consciousness.

When people are committed together in this way, each person continuously is evolving into a new dimension of his being. Each continuously can be falling in love with the new elements recognized in himself and the other.

The polarities of the two partners become so perfectly aligned that they form a conduit through which cosmic energy or love begins to flow. The greater love force takes over and expresses each of them as personalities, yet they transcend the personalities.

Unfortunately, most marriages remain at a level of plodding through fears and insecurities, working out compromises based on emotions that intimidate, clutch and possess. They seldom move into the dynamic flow of love energy that unites and enlivens both partners.

The Homosexual Marriage

There are a lot of viewpoints about the homosexual marriage, whether between two women or two men. My channel has said that any union in love is okay in the eyes of God. Remember that no one is strictly homosexual or heterosexual, and no one should be forced into playing a role that he or she is not comfortable with. As we are ready we evolve into the roles we need, deciding what is best for our continuing growth in sensitivity and understanding.

So, if a male homosexual needs a feminine balance, he will draw to him a feminine man. If he needs a more masculine balance, he will draw the more masculine man. We draw to us what we need to balance our energies no matter what sex role we are playing out. Again, the most important thing in any relationship, whether homosexual or heterosexual, is the love bond and the commitment between the two individuals, to grow together in unfolding their highest potentials. We are responsible for using or not using our God given talents, not whether we have had homosexual or heterosexual alliances.

My channel has said that the aligning of energy between two entities of the same sex in a particular incarnation is not as powerful as the aligning of energies of opposite sexes. But the energy is powerful enough and there is nothing wrong with the union—it is not less important or less valid. They have explained that they are not endorsing rampant homosexuality, because then there would be no opportunity for souls to incarnate on the earth plane. But some entities for a particular incarnation feel more comfortable in working out their karma with a member of the same sex.

The biggest problem with homosexuality is the rise of the gay movement in which there is much partner swapping and jumping from person to person. It is much more difficult to keep a homosexual union going than a heterosexual, because as I mentioned the combined energy is not as strong. The partner swapping of the gays is still a result of the "something is missing" feeling, which can be discovered only when one decides to commit to another person and balance his energies within. I have counseled with many homosexuals who have difficulty handling a full-time relationship. I also have talked with many who are disenchanted with the gay movement because they feel they are thought of as "nothing more than a slab of meat. The guys aren't interested in who I really am, my thoughts and feelings." It is the same story, whether heterosexual swinging or homosexual swinging. We all have the inner desire to unite, to merge and be completely known by another. After a while anything less than that loses its meaning and importance.

The Time Investment

The true marriage takes a great deal of work to achieve. Generally we need from 9-14 years to develop this kind of attunement and oneness. It is through our daily commitment to working on a relationship and our own self-growth that we move into this space of fulfillment and unity within ourselves and with another. But many marriages have gone down the drain long before that time, and the persons involved never really knew what marriage was supposed to be about.

My channel recommends spending the first three years together building your own relationship, minus children, although many of us don't have these ideal circumstances. But those of you who haven't gotten into a partnership or marriage yet and can make that choice, realize that those first three years can make a lot of difference in whether or not your union lasts. They will contribute immensely to your psychological balance and communication with your partner, and more fully prepare you for children when they do arrive.

This doesn't mean that if you already have children you shouldn't remarry, but it does mean that all persons in the family situation will have to work harder to keep their energy up, communication lines open, and heads clear. When I asked my channel about the timing for children coming into the marriage union, they explained:

"We definitely say people should wait three years before having children. This is because the first three years are a crucial period for setting up the marriage union. They determine how it's going to go. Actually the first year you are setting up a program of relating that you will follow for the rest of that marriage unless one or the other becomes aware enough to break the program. It is much more difficult to break a habit than to build one. The first three years are very important, then, just as the first three years of a child's life. You owe it to yourself and your partner to spend this time balancing your energies together, learning one another's areas of strength and weakness, and being supportive of one another's growth.

"If you start with children you'll discover that there is not the time, the energy or the clarity to see what the other person's needs are. And if you haven't set a firm, solid foundation you won't know one another.

"In days past this was fine when people had jobs assigned to them, a particular role to play. Your culture was primarily agrarian, and couples who married and lived on a farm assigned roles to all their children, almost from the day they were born. Even city dwellers assigned roles to both themselves and their children in terms of taking over the family business, or learning a skill from the father or mother. You knew what was expected of you and often there was hardship and struggle just to survive. There was not an identity crisis then as there is today, which made interpersonal relationships simpler.

In today's generation individuals must work much harder and invest a lot more energy in exploring and understanding who they really are. The soul must learn whether it is the breadwinner, the parent, the partner, or a combination. The individual soul must blend a variety of roles together in its own consciousness, which makes it much harder and more difficult in establishing a marriage union, blending these energies together. You are having to learn how to give your partner independence to follow his or her own leading, and at the same time join in a loving, caring and supportive union. It is very difficult at this particular stage in your evolution to learn how to blend self-growth and independence within the bond of marriage. That is exactly why so many marriages are collapsing."

Sharing Your Stereotypes

Each of us enters the marriage relationship with masculine and feminine stereotypes and ideas of the ideal husband or wife. We often expect our partner immediately to conform to our images of the perfect mate, satisfy all our needs and be there whenever we need him. A helpful exercise in communication is to share these stereotypes with your partner. Compare images, and see where they conform to or depart from the expectations of the other. By doing this you also begin to realize the absurdity and limitations of these predetermined images, especially if you are going to share roles and learn to express both the masculine and feminine sides of your individual natures.

Don't go into a marriage with unrealistic notions. Each of us constantly is changing and moving through different patterns of growth. Our ability to respond and be sensitive to our mates varies with our energy levels and awareness. Often when you feel hurt by your partner, he is totally unaware of the situation. Pouting and closing off solves nothing. Openly communicate where your head is, and this will enable you to look at any expectations or stereotyped images that haven't been fulfilled. In this way we can let go of the old programs, and our partners can help us by being more sensitive to what we are working with.

Problems in Communication

Another major difficulty in communicating with our partners is that we often forget there's more than just a one-to-one relationship between husband and wife. Each of us has a critic or parent vibration, a playful child vibe, and an adult or mature vibe. So there's three of me and three of my husband, and all three of us get together and communicate. If my husband is talking from his child space, and I'm coming from my parent space, then that's a real put-down for him. His creativity is evaluated rather than enjoyed and explored. He would be hurting because of that and might not even know why. He may be playing and kidding, and I'm saying how stupid you are, why don't you grow up. I'm destroying his fun and imagination. We shouldn't even be critics or judges of our own childlike behavior, because we have to allow ourselves to play without putting us down. For example, when your partner is being the child, allow your inner child to come out too, and play and laugh together. So many people forget how to be children again. They become so engrossed and uptight over their jobs and other daily concerns that stress and tension build up significantly. They drop dead of heart attacks or suffer from physical or mental disturbances.

Be careful of playing the parental role with one another. Women, I've found, are especially guilty of this. If we play the mother role for our husbands, it's a cop out because it puts us in the manipulative position. They really need us because we handle everything, take care of them and give advice. This gives us power, and it seems much safer than opening up to a relationship of mutually shared responsibility, adult to adult or man to woman. When either partner continuously plays the parent it will weaken the other one. Any of us will slide if we can, and we will let others make our decisions for us and lean on them. But that isn't growing, and it will eventually prove dehabilitating to one aspect or another of the relationship.

The Family

The loving and supportive family unit always has been the strength of any society. My teachers have explained that when the concept of the family falls apart, our country will also fall apart. This is one of the reasons that the message of commitment to grow together and provide models for our children is so crucial today. The family represents a microcosmic universe, the basic unit in which growth is gained through working out karmic ties with individuals and which in turn prepares us for our adult roles. The family provides the medium for children to learn how to stick-to-it, to look at and work through problems taking into consideration both their own needs and the needs of others around them. Learning to love and work with others with diverse personalities gives the child the stability to work through problems that arise within his own marriage, job situation, or any other life experience later on.

My channel states: "If children see the family degenerating, each person going off on his own to do his or her own thing, if they see the random splitting up and diversification of energies minus the love commitment, they will not know how to work through situations in their own lives and will constantly be running from any confrontation or unpleasant-ness. The purpose of an incarnation is not to avoid unpleas-antness, but to understand why it is so and to change the situation into one of harmony.

"The family constitutes the child's first beginnings in under-standing how to work together, how to cope with and handle diversity, how to handle failure and financial struggle. In the family children can really begin to learn that teamwork is involved in every situation, whether it is cleaning up a yard or handling a particular emergency that arises for one of its members. The family is the place to learn about the caring of individual people and people as a group, and that all things can be worked out in understanding and love.

"At times you may not like a member of the family, or may not like a decision that other family members have made. Here you learn how to accept an individual whether you agree with him or not, and how to work with others for the good of everyone concerned.

"At the heart of the family is learning how to experience and give unconditional love. The child learns that no matter what he does, he is going to be loved by the parents. He learns that nothing is so bad he does or experiences that he cannot confide in his parents. Instead of meeting with hostility and rejection he meets with total love and understanding, and the support he needs to work through the situation. This love and support is learned in your youth as you are growing up. It is much more difficult to learn this as an adult, and many never do. They build their relationships on insecurity and fear.

"One of the biggest problems in your country today is that so many who have reached adulthood have not had this unconditional love as children. They have never learned the meaning of true love and caring. Robbery, murder and violent efforts to change the system result from persons having no foundation in love.

"Many persons who are searching to better mankind and themselves are doing so using violent tactics. They don't know how to accomplish their goal, to truly bring harmony within the existing order of things. To establish order in your world and the universe you must begin by bringing order to yourself, in your perspective, in your thinking and attitudes. People trying to better the world without a foundation in love are doing it from selfish perspectives. They have forgotten that balance comes from within. If this kind of harmony is not taught within the family situation, where are your children going to learn it? They must learn as youth how to bring order out of chaos, harmony out of disharmony, using love."

Remembering to Nurture Your One-to-One Relationship

What most nourishes love within our children is the nurturing of love within ourselves. If the relationship with our partner is dynamic and supportive, it will provide an ideal growth environment for our children. Almost every counseling situation I have encountered in which the parents are complaining about the child's behavior is actually reflecting disharmony between the parents. On some level the child feels a lack of acceptance, misunderstood or unloved, and by the same token has not been taught responsibility for self and others.

To ensure harmonious functioning on all levels you should be willing to invest time in enhancing your relationship with your partner. At least every four to six weeks get away for a weekend by yourselves and laugh and play together, keeping the romance alive in your marriage. "We can't afford it" or "We shouldn't leave the children" are poor excuses for not taking this important time to give to your relationship. If nothing else you can take sleeping bags and camp out, and can make a reciprocal arrangement with friends or relatives for keeping the children.

But in addition to your weekend away, it is important to sit down for just a few minutes every night after the kids are in bed. This is what I call "C and C time," compliments and criticism time. Really communicate to your partner what's happening inside you. Your partner should be your best friend. Find out what each of you is thinking, where you're at. If you have been hurt by something, or have been feeling left out or rejected, say that. If your partner has been nagging you, you should express that feeling, too. Also, compliment each other on at least one thing you liked or appreciated that the other one did, even if it was nothing more than a smile or a kind word. You should communicate anything that's been pushing your buttons, whether it concerns your sex life or who leaves the cap off the toothpaste. Most important, don't forget to touch and hold one another. Touching and hugging gives energy, aligns your energy fields and renews you in one another's caring. Too many marriages forget this very important aspect. If you don't naturally hold and hug one another each day, you are isolating yourselves from the attunement and energy you both deserve, and your relationship needs some improvement.

The Importance of Your Own Space

Even though we are working on blending energies with our partner in the marriage union, we never want to lose the sense of our own unique worth as a person. A man came in to talk to me who recently had been divorced. He was greatly depressed, after having been married for 20 years. His wife had asked for the separation. He explained, "All my life I have seen myself through the eyes of my wife. I didn't think of me apart from her, and my successes and failures were evaluated in terms of how she responded." This man was successful in the professional world, but he had never developed a sense of who he was, and his sense of self-esteem was coming from without—his wife—rather than from within. The marriage broke up because he had to learn how to stand on his own two feet, to have feelings and opinions of his own, and to realize that what he gives and receives in a relationship is valuable because he happens to be a unique person.

In our togetherness we must find time to be alone. Just as we must give the partnership time alone, away from the kids to revitalize itself, so we must give the self as an individual unit time alone to revitalize and renew.

Often when I get home from work at night I'll tell my kids that I'm tired and need some time to myself before I begin preparing dinner. They give me my space, and I go outside and dig in the garden, putter around the yard, and tune out the day. I am communing with nature, and restoring my energies. I also have hobbies that I work on by myself when I need to play alone, relax with myself and not be concerned with relating to anyone else. I work with ceramics, and do jigsaw puzzles.

When I am in a space where I need time alone, my kids and husband are very understanding. If I need to take an hour to myself, I let them know that's what I'm doing. If you want to be alone, or need some time to yourself, no one will be uptight or feel rejected as long as you communicate to them what you're doing. For example, my husband will say to me, "Honey, I love you, and I'm taking my hour now," or "I'm going to spend some time alone, now." An important thing to teach your children is how to respect other people's private space and not feel threatened or unloved by it. It I were always at their beck and call they would not develop self-reliance or an appreciation of other people's needs. All it takes is the verbalization of where your head is and why you need some space. It is being considerate of others and yourself. Again, it is the quality of time we spend with one another rather than the amount. If a mother is with her children all day but tunes them out because she is tired or preoccupied, it isn't nearly as effective in terms of building a productive relationship as if the parent spends only a few hours with the child but gives him total attention and a genuine sense of caring and love.

Swinging: Problems and Value

I continuously have mentioned the importance of the one-to-one relationship in building the most effective union for interpersonal and self-growth. My channel consistently maintains that in a true marriage, a heart-to-heart union, there would be no desire within either partner to have outside sexual relationships. This doesn't mean that you don't love other people. But often people feel that if you love someone else, whether man or woman, you must have a sexual expression of this love. And this is where the love is misunderstood, because we truly can love and experience all people from our higher spiritual centers, with no accompanying desire or need to have sexual relationships with them.

My channel has said: "No marriage can exist with one partner being unfaithful, even if the other partner gives permission. It's not going to work. Sooner or later it is going to cause a hurt and heartache to one or both partners. It brings an imbalance in the union."

The heart-to-heart commitment, they explain, "is that commitment for better or for worse, to work together to unfold and to manifest the God-consciousness individually and collectively, to manifest the greatest awareness, the greatest talents, abilities, and to achieve the greatest growth possible together in this lifetime. This is why true marriage has seldom been tried. And few have reaped the rewards of the total joy of the true marriage union.

"To diversify energy means the relationship will suffer. Many marriages, for example, begin to fall apart at the seams when the first children come along, because children take a lot of energy and the couple has not built the needed base ahead of time. If you think of how diversified your energy is with your children, can you not understand that if you are directing the sexual energy toward other couples or another partner you are spreading yourselves too thin? To direct your sexual energies away from your marriage relationship means that you are undermining the stability of the love bond that you should be developing in the relationship."

Not too long ago a priest announced that extramarital affairs in some cases could save a marriage, and were necessary to the survival of marriages in our day and age. When I asked the channel about the validity of the priest's comments, they replied: "He's missing the point. He's working in order to keep Christianity's traditional view of the marriage in tact. Divorce in the Catholic Church has been considered quite serious, you know. He is trying to give couples an out to keep up the marriage front, for the sake of the children, by suggesting that extramarital affairs are okay. He isn't realizing that those outside affairs are not the answer. What is missing in a marriage will not be found in an outside relationship. Temporary sexual satisfaction, perhaps, but in the casual outside affair there is not the deep and total commitment to loving one another."

Recently it seems that 90 per cent of my counseling has been marriage counseling. I am continuously amazed at the number of people who have lovers on the side. What an easy ego stroke, to enjoy a few romantic hours with your lover devoid of any other responsibility. But if you had to live with your lover 24 hours a day, he might not look quite as romantic. Women whose husbands turn them off turn to an outside lover rather than working through the problem, and the same with men. But the real test of growth is facing the situation and learning to blend the romance, work, love and responsibility into a relationship far more beautiful than we ever imagined. A number of women have told me that the lover relationship is really the most satisfying answer to their life situation. The husband's making a living, their children are taken care of, and they don't have to make waves at home. They have an acceptable social position, and why should they change that? Likewise, the men who have lovers say they don't want to give up the wife and mother of their children, their established social standing in the community, and they don't have to make advances to their wife who really doesn't enjoy sex anyway.

What neither party understands is that you will never get your marriage going if your need for love and caring is being fulfilled outside the marriage. The lover or mistress thing is simple. You can always replace it, and there are plenty of people to fill the bill. And we've got to understand that most of us have been programmed to think the grass is always greener on the other side of the fence.

But that is not really getting in and growing. No matter what age we are, we all want to be loved, and we have to be honest about what our needs are. Many women I talk with are having outside affairs just because they want to be touched or held, not particularly because they want the sex part of the relationship. We all thrive on being touched and hugged, whether we realize it or not, because it is an exchange of energy.

Once when I was giving the "Sex and Psychic Energy" lecture a young man asked me about a particular situation involving some friends of his. "What do you think about a marriage situation which both partners enjoy, both agree they can have outside relationships, and neither one is jealous?" To this I let my channel answer, and they replied: "This is not a marriage. These people love and respect each other to a degree, and it is a comfortable relationship, but it is not a heart-to-heart love. This is rather a comforting intellectual situation. Each one knows that he has someone when the need arises, and someone with whom to share responsibilities and to work. But they have no true commitment when it comes to working on their own growth. They are prisoners within their own framework, although they think they are trying to do their own thing."

I talked with one woman who had four men. One was her lover, one her intellectual companion, one enjoyed the opera with her, and the other played like a kid with her. She asked me, "Is there anything wrong with having four?" And I said, "No. You can have as many friends as you like. There's nothing wrong with that. But understand that you're copping out from making an in-depth commitment to any one person which would accelerate your own growth even more." You see, if any one of the four didn't want to do what she wanted, she just replaced them. She didn't want a commitment because she was afraid of getting involved and getting hurt. She was able to use these people for her own needs, which was very selfish. You're not really going to learn much from having that kind of relationship, except that finally it isn't enough.

My channel also emphasizes that various sexual experiences, having an affair or swinging, should not be judged as "good" or "bad." They are simply experiences that we have set up to help us learn something about ourselves. But bringing a third or fourth party into the marriage alliance will scatter the energy and will move the relationship away from its goal of God-union. Both men and women have been programmed until very recently with the so-called double standard in marriage. It is all right for men to have extra affairs and a roving eye, but not women. But men are no more highly sexed than women are, and this is merely a macho role they consciously or subconsciously play out because they think it is expected of them. God meant for both the man and the woman to enjoy sex equally. Boredom can set in any relationship if two people aren't working on their own growth and improving the quality of their responses to one another. Boredom, however, results from second chakra sex, not the dynamic heart to heart union. Second chakra sex constantly looks for new thrills, and seeks the ultimate penis or the ultimate vagina. But the ultimate is truly knowing the self, and no experience will prove to be *enough* until that inner attunement is established.

Remember that you can choose to do anything you want, and that's okay. Any experience is just for your learning. In other words, it's okay to choose to cop out if you want to, but just don't kid yourself about what's really going on. Don't feel guilty if you don't want to commit yourself to a full-time relationship, but acknowledge that you're choosing it, and learn the most that you can from what you are doing. Eventually, we've all got to get in and work on that one-to-one.

Dropping Roles and Sharing Needs

Being a psychic has its advantages in counseling. When people come into my office they presume that I already know everything about them anyway so they level with me. They aren't afraid to tell me where they're really coming from. And often I think how easy their relationships would be at home if they would do the same thing with their spouses. There is no need to play a role with the person you love. When you drop the role, you drop all the anxiety and uncertainty that goes with it.

So many women have told me, "My husband doesn't love me any more." When I ask why do they think that, they answer, "He doesn't touch me," or hold me, or do this and that. I ask them if they tell him what their needs are. "Do you ask him to hold you? Do you tell him you *want* to be touched and held? Do you create a positive and supportive environment in which he would feel free to do this?"

Usually they have neglected to mention anything about this to their husbands. "No, he's just supposed to do it." The husband may be totally unaware that the wife desires additional affection, or that she is feeling rejected or unloved. It may be that at some earlier time or two he made advances and the wife seemed too busy or uninterested, and he didn't want to run the risk of rejection again. Most of us have extremely sensitive egos. This is why it is so crucial to tell each other about our needs. If you care about one another your partner is usually more than willing to work with you, and probably is delighted that you desire to work on improving the affectional level of your relationship.

I once counseled with a business man who was on the verge of killing himself. He had become an alcoholic from the tension and pressure of his work. He was trying to provide his wife with every material thing she asked for. For seven years he had been robbing from Peter to pay Paul, and was just on the verge of breaking when I met him. I asked him if he had ever sat down and frankly told her that he couldn't afford something, that he flat out didn't have it, and ask her what she suggested that they do. He said no, that he never told her he didn't have the money to buy something that she wanted because he was afraid that she would no longer love him.

First of all, this man was suffering from a very low self-image that said "I am not worthy of my wife's love." Second, he was being terribly unrealistic and was playing out a long-embedded macho role that said he had to be the great provider-stud-father for his wife who stayed at home all day. I explained that he simply would have to level with her. If she wanted to work and bring in additional income for the extras, fine. But that if not, they would have to cut back accordingly. I was trying to tell him not to be afraid to share responsibilities. If your partner wants *things* rather than love, and you choose to stay in that relationship, you will be miserable. But you don't have to stay. And when you know that you deserve love, mutual concern, teamwork and growth, then you'll have it. The man cried for a long time, and began to realize he had held too much in for too long.

If I feel scared or down in the dumps, I may say to my husband, "Just hold me for a few minutes, will you?" I'm not asking him to resolve my problem. If I feel supported and loved, if I get that extra boost of energy and relax about it, I'll get my own answer. Also, if you just feel that something is wrong and you don't know what it is, ask your partner to sit down and talk with you about it. When you begin to talk about your feelings, get them up and out, you'll find out what's going on. The other person never has to handle it for you. Don't get stuck in the bind of thinking you have to solve your partner's problems. We are all very jealous of our own problems, and not only do we basically *want* to solve them ourselves, but we *have* to solve them ourselves. Your partner merely serves as a sounding board for you to hear yourself.

Working Through Sex Hang-ups

"Both partners come into this lifetime with certain hang-ups and perspectives on sex, and acquire many more during their upbringing," says my channel. "But if people meditate together, if they converse honestly from their hearts, there would be no problems in marriage or in sex."

More women are sexually unfulfilled than men. Women only recently have begun to learn what their potential for sexual experience really is, and that it is okay to communicate their sexual needs. The partner, no matter how beautiful and sensitive he may be, does not know what is in your heart unless you open up and verbalize this. Many women have sexual fantasies and get some fulfillment from that, rather than confronting their real needs and expressing them to their mates. Fantasizing is fine and a healthy release which many people need in order to let go of inner tensions, but how much better it is when two people can sit down together, heart to heart and face to face, and admit the problems they're having in their sexual union. Honest communication opens doors to genuine problem solving and undreamed of new heights in experience together. You have entered the marriage in order to learn, not cover up what you aren't experiencing or don't understand. It takes years to build a lasting sexual union, and it must begin through open communication. Otherwise, you will wind up with nothing.

All too often women have labeled themselves frigid or blocked because they have tried to find sexual release or experience orgasm and have been unable to do so. Consequently, they give up. But resentment and feeling cheated are negative emotions which build a wall between you and your partner. These blocks and frustrations should be openly discussed with your partner, and both should begin to work with techniques given in Chapter 5. Mental attitudes are of crucial importance. Remember that you always can solve any problem, sexual or otherwise. We simply have to realize that we have the potential to do so, and not feel embarrassed about asking questions and looking at what is limiting us from our achievement.

Both people should sit down together and talk of ways to enhance their relationship. This should be a time when it is quiet and no one will disturb you. Whoever approaches the subject or brings it up does not have to do it in the context of "I am sexually unfulfilled," but rather "Let's talk about ways we can make our marriage better, and more completely satisfying to each of us." If the vibe is truly non-threatening and loving, it will not offend the other person's ego. If the woman needs more tenderness or more foreplay, she should communicate this. And if the man feels that he needs more understanding or support in the relationship, he should communicate that.

If a woman enjoys tenderness and touching and the man has never learned to give it (or vice versa) it will help both of them to learn to experience this together. But the partner who is accustomed to the caring and tenderness will need to be very patient and very strong, because it is too easy to feel rejected and unloved because one's mate doesn't come by affection "naturally." Men who learn the joy of touching and tenderness are greatly enhancing their total experience. We must think of the entire body as a vehicle for expression and pleasure.

If a woman has been faking orgasms or if the man doesn't realize it is important for her to have one, both should level with each other here, too. I'm surprised at the number of women who fake orgasms, from age 17-80, and who seldom have a genuine feeling of sexual completion.

Both people should be very clear on how they feel about their own body and their partner's body. Any do's and don'ts you have about your personal sex life may be strong inhibitions which are greatly limiting both yourself and your partner. If you think parts of the body are dirty, or that parts are unacceptable, you will not convey an attitude of delight and acceptance in your mate.

A lot of people have hang-ups about oral sex. That's how they were brought up. I know many men who go to prostitutes or other women just because they want oral sex and their wives won't give it to them. And I know some men who greatly enjoy their wives giving them oral sex but won't reciprocate. If you're uptight you have to look at those attitudes. The body is clean and is a beautiful thing, to be loved, experienced and enjoyed.

If we could learn to keep communication open between us, there would be no need for clinics, psychiatrists and prostitutes. But all serve a valuable purpose in the condition of our present society.

Understanding Divorce

Many reasons are given for divorces, the most common being sexual incompatibility. But the real reason behind all the rest is lack of communication. Good sex begins with good communication.

In a divorce it is never one partner's "fault." There are always patterns of behavior contributed by both parties that create tension in the relationship. So it is a fallacy to think of straightening out one person and then having the marriage work. It is a matter of treating the relationship, not the individuals. A relationship is a dynamic field of energies, taking on a life of its own. It is looking at these intermingling energy patterns that gives us a clue to what both people need to work on, collectively and individually.

Again, when things begin to get tough we are only too quick to discuss our problems in the context of "It's all your fault. How could you do this?" We never stop to look at the inherent lesson involved for each of us in the situation, and how we set it up in the first place.

A couple who had been married for almost seven years seemingly had good communication and a meaningful relationship. But suddenly the relationship began to deteriorate rapidly. This, we might initially think, doesn't fit the rules. When the husband sat down one night and told his wife he was considering divorce, she burst into tears and replied, "I always thought someday you'd leave me." She didn't understand how the mind works and the things we fear, even hidden away in our hearts, we must face or eliminate completely from our thinking processes. She really had not faced a lot of the difficulties she saw in the marriage because of fear of making waves and losing her husband. Karmically, if two people are drawn together and they both continue to grow and communicate, there is no need for them ever to split up. They would never have to leave the relationship. But in our generation we have unlimited possibilities to play many roles and work in many different fields, and communication is essential to keep abreast of where the other person is at. If the growth together stops, sure, we have to get up and get out. The whole key is we've got to grow.

At the first signs of difficulty the couple should seek help from a professional counselor, or either openly discuss and look at their own problems together. All too often couples wait until they literally hate each other, and the love they shared for each other is gone. Then it is too late. You should never be fearful of counseling and seeking the help that you need. But it is better not to talk about your marital problems with everyone on the neighborhood gossip circuit, because then you merely accentuate them without seeing how you both have set them up. You also betray the confidence of your mate, and are in effect saying, "I'm willing to communicate with everyone but you." If you can tell someone else what is bothering you about your relationship, you should be able to tell your mate the same thing.

A One-Way Street

If your partner's attitude is "It's you who's all messed up, not me," and he won't go into counseling with you, then there is nothing you can do about that attitude. You can decide to stay in the situation and get satisfaction from things other than the relationship, or you can say that you love yourself enough to know you don't deserve that. Anyone who tells you it's your problem and he is going to continue doing his own thing in his own way is copping out. He has no intention of building the kind of relationship that will enhance both partners.

When You Decide to Divorce

Obviously one should not stay in a destructive relationship. My channel has said, "It must be stressed that you know within your hearts that you have tried everything humanly and divinely possible to keep the marriage together. For it is not by accident that you find yourselves in a marriage union. It is important to know, however, that once you have given your all, and still cannot overcome the difficulty, due to the other person's or your own refusal to work and grow, then for your own soul's development the union should be ended."

Another will be led into your life to help your growth continue. If one partner is constantly pulling the other down, if one partner does not wish to work on building constuctive habits, then you should have the wisdom to leave. But your own motives and desires for wanting to leave the situation must be surveyed very objectively, with prayer and forethought. You should realize the reasons for leaving, and the problems that were not solved. You must examine why you attracted these problems to you in the first place, and what programs of fear and insecurity you have been running.

We must know that we have tried to make the union work, have given it our best, before we leave. And we can get clarity on whether to leave by asking through prayer, listening to our guidance in a meditative state, or asking that the answer be given to us in a dream. If you are earnestly seeking to do what is best for both you and your partner, you will be shown the way.

I've worked with a number of people who are married to alcoholics. Alcoholics are very psychic and sensitive and can't handle drugs or alcohol. They don't know how to tune out other people's vibes, so they begin drinking to dull their senses and enable them to relax. The alcoholic always has a choice of whether he or she wants to stay in that miserable world or get out. And if you're married to an alcoholic you have the same choice. If you have explored many avenues of help, your partner doesn't try or keeps slipping back, for you it's like watching a child destroy himself, and there's nothing you can do in your frustration. You have to ask yourself several things: Why am I staying in the relationship? Do I feel like I deserve this? Am I playing the parent role so I will feel needed? Do I think I can help, when I really know that no one can do it for us? Do I think my partner would destroy himself if I left? Your partner is destroying himself and you anyway, so that last question really doesn't hold a lot of meaning.

We must realize that there is no way we can love someone enough to get them to change if they don't want to. They may say they want to change, but if they aren't seeking help then they are continuing to use the habit of addiction as a cop out and a tool for manipulation. If I don't want your help there is no way you can help. Even God won't go against our free will. The only way for me to really learn is to do it myself. So the hard part is, if you really loved me you'd dump me and let me crash. And then when I'm down there wallowing in my misery I can choose to stay down or say, "Hey, I don't need it." Then I'll decide to fight my way out because I really want it.

But the greatest gift you could give me is to leave me. Ultimately we all have to develop that inner strength to make it on our own. Real love is standing by you, helping you see what the lesson is, but not doing it for you. We can't take anyone else up the mountain of life but ourselves. Each and every one of us has to learn how to walk up on our own. If I try to do it for you, I'm weakening you and you become dependent on me. Then, even if subconsciously, you begin to hate me because I've shown you your weaknesses and am keeping you down by playing the parent.

We have heard countless times that we can't change anybody but ourselves. Yet most of us don't really believe it.

So many women marry thinking that all their man needs is a lot of love and then he'll change. Or vice versa. But the only person you have a right to change is yourself, and the only person you *can* change is yourself. Attempts to remake the other are manipulation, and aren't genuine change, growth, or insight for the other from within. Where your partner is and what he is doing is fine for him. If you can walk together, beautiful, and if you can't, let go and let God. God will lead someone else into your life and someone else into your partner's life.

My channel also has pointed out that sometimes divorce "comes as a result or a culmination of working out the karma between two people. If there is no more karma then the soul is free to leave, or to make a joint decision with his partner to continue growing in new directions with one another." But all too often the "I've worked through my karma with him" attitude is given as an excuse not to face what is really there to be learned in the first place.

Another great cop out for leaving a partnership I often hear, especially from women, is "I've met my true soul mate, and it is only right that we should be together." But these same people soon want to jump out of their new relationships when they indeed meet the next soul mate, and the next. In the first place, you would never incarnate at the same time with your true soul mate. Your counterpart is walking with you through the incarnation, and you in turn walk with him—out of the body. We meet many people we feel very attuned to from past life experiences. We have, in that sense, a universe of soul mates. But the person you have formed a partnership with is not someone to leave on the spur of the moment. If you don't work through it you'll have to come back in another lifetime to do it.

Divorce Isn't Easy

Divorce is never easy. Many times you experience a tremendous energy drop and go into a state of depression. Part of this is because the other person, even in a bad relationship, has been an energy source for you and now is gone. Our first reaction is usually to blame the other person. Then we swing into a heavy self-guilt number. "It's all my fault, how terrible I've been." We vascillate back and forth, from self blame to partner blame, from depression to moments of feeling relieved and quite free. The first thing to remember to do is get outdoors, get plenty of exercise and fresh air, and keep your energy up. Make it a point to be around happy and creative people. Do anything from watching children playing in a park to "people watching" in a shopping center. Don't allow yourself to hang around with those who want you to go into the gory details and listen to how terrible you're feeling. Get involved in some creative project, something completely new that you've never done before.

It is very important to continue meditating, and begin to work on your own head. Begin to reexamine in a very objective way the trips and programs that were not satisfactory in your previous marriage, the things that were satisfactory, and what you need to work on in yourself so that you can contribute to building a fulfilling relationship with your next partner. List your goals, and your needs. Begin to write positive suggestions for yourself and visualize your goals as realities. You need to spend some time evaluating what you really want, and how you need to clean up your act. Think of this particular period in your life as a splendid opportunity for learning, and working through, perhaps some of your most important lessons in this lifetime. It is usually best not to jump immediately into a new marriage until you've had time to really evaluate the old, or you may set up the same thing all over again. If you're in touch with your inner self you will have a sense of guidance and will know when it is right for you to establish a new relationship. Each person must move at his or her own pace. But you can save yourself a lot of grief and trauma if you take an active interest in the divorce process as a marvelous learning opportunity, and practice working on forgiving and sending love to all in your life who need it.

Summary

Remember that the secret of a happy marriage is communication. This means communicating not only your joys and pleasures, but also your fears and insecurities. Anything not shared becomes a block. When we can share our negative programs (as well as our positive) in a spirit of trust, looking at them and changing them, we can grow very fast indeed.

The true marriage relationship has seldom been tried. It remains a frontier of love and freedom within our own inner being, and still awaits our exploration.

Chapter 5

Techniques
To Enhance
Sexual Sensitivity

In recent years sex technique manuals have flourished. They have served a useful purpose because many of us were lacking basic knowledge in the varieties of sexual behavior. But many have suggested that if you knew the right position, discovered your erogenous zones, or learned a number of methods, your sexual problems would be over.

What so often has been forgotten is the intricate emotional and psychological make-up of the individual which determines *how* he responds to even the slightest touch. Sex and the enjoyment of sex is much more a mind-set than a technique. It is our attitudes and beliefs that either block or open us to experiencing energy throughout our bodies. And no one is responsible for heightening sexual awareness within an individual but the individual himself. We are responsible for our own orgasms, exploring our mental hang-ups, and asking our partners to work with us.

It is helpful to remember that there is virtually no such thing as a sexual problem that cannot be solved. Current medical research, sex therapy clinics, self-discovery techniques, meditation, and various sexual aids enable us to work through almost anything if we really want to.

When we refuse to work on the sexual dimension of ourselves, we are inhibiting one aspect of our spiritual progress. Understanding ourselves sexually will have to be worked out in either this or a future incarnation.

Looking at Sexual Hang-ups

No matter what gender or sex role we happen to be in at the moment, we probably have some blocks about sex that are limiting our total experience. We may wish to seek professional help, but often this is not necessary when we begin to be honest with ourselves, perhaps for the first time.

Ask yourself what your attitudes are, how you feel about your body and your partner's body. Do you feel any part of the male or female body is unclean? Does any part repulse you? Do you feel you are unworthy to be loved sexually? Do you fear rejection or that you won't please your partner? Begin to explore your sexual programming, reflect on the attitudes you learned from your parents, and consider how they may be impairing or enhancing your sex life today. Also, we bring with us into this life attitudes from past incarnations. For example, a person who has just spent an incarnation in a monastery may be more comfortable playing the counselor instead of the lover. But regardless of our attitudes, no matter what they are or where we acquired them, we have the power to change them by learning to love ourselves as we really are—beautiful expressions of infinite energy.

Releasing Hang-Ups about Your Body

Perhaps you have some hang-ups about your body. Most people do, thinking they are either too fat or too skinny, out of proportion, and so on. If you are shy and afraid to be seen in the nude by your partner, relax and try the following exercise: Imagine that your body is turning into pure energy. Experience yourself in a totally fluid state, tuning into yourself as an energy being. Mentally repeat that this is the love energy, the creative energy of God. Then imagine that this energy is once again assuming the shape of your own body, but in the place of the old body you now feel and sense a new form that is a special creation of love. Picture and feel this new body as one which deserves love and should be given love, one that is able to both give and receive. You are mentally creating a new image of yourself. It is vital that you understand your physical vehicle in this way, for then you are able to overcome many inhibitions and realize more fully the purpose of the body you have chosen.

If it has been a long time since you looked at yourself in a mirror completely nude, try it when no one else is around to disturb you. Examine your body as if you were seeing it for the first time. Pretend you've never seen a body before, and admire your own as a unique creation. Notice the curves, textures, hair, temperature, everything. Then tell yourself that this is your special vehicle, made in the image of God, and that your body is beautiful. Practice repeating, "My body is beautiful" for awhile. Begin to see your body as the physical expression of your spirit. People don't love you for your body, they love you for your spirit, your vibrations. And as *you* learn to love your own body and the spiritual self within, both body and spirit become more beautiful.

Common Sexual Problems

Three of the most common labels for sexual dysfunction are premature ejaculation, frigidity and impotence. They all can be overcome because they result from mental blocks and not knowing how to properly channel energy through the human system (unless, of course, one suffers from some critical physical infirmity).

Frigidity and impotence have common roots. The energy is blocked from flowing into the second chakra because of negative mental programs, either conscious or subconscious. Impotence, for example, may be brought on by doubting one's masculinity, fear of inability to perform, or old programs that sex is dirty or unclean. It also can result from worry over any situation with which one associates a sense of self-worth, such as a job, finances, or interpersonal relationships. Impotence can be brought on by an unresponsive wife who suffers from the Victorian ethics that a woman is just supposed to lie there and receive. If a man feels his wife is simply accommodating him, he may soon get turned off and be unable to get an erection.

The frigid woman who thinks she cannot have an orgasm may have learned years ago to turn off sexually when she got too excited on a date. Or, if she does not really love and trust her partner, she may be subconsciously holding back, not wanting to give herself completely because she doesn't love completely. She may be caught in the vicious circle of building up excitement, getting worried that she won't reach a climax soon enough and her partner will get tired, and then turning off so she won't be disappointed. But most cases of frigidity result from not learning how to awaken and experience energy in the second chakra, or from general ignorance of the fact that women have the potential for orgasm.

I've counseled many women of all ages who consider themselves frigid and consequently fake orgasms. Faking orgasms cheats both parties, and really isn't necessary. Even if you've done it for years, and you're afraid you'll hurt your partner by suddenly being honest, it is best to lay your cards on the table in a spirit of love. Explain to your partner what's been happening to you, that you really didn't understand it before, and ask for his help. Then the partner can respond to you without feeling threatened. Chances are, he has not been fully enjoying the relationship either because he sensed something was missing (your energy) but didn't know what. You must love and trust enough to communicate your feelings. Your partner wants to know that he truly gives pleasure to you, so tell him where you are.

Learning to have an orgasm is really quite simple if you begin to work alone with a vibrator, and there are many varieties on the market today. Take a nice hot bath, relax, and then lie down where you won't be disturbed. Don't run thoughts through your mind of "What am I doing? This is ridiculous!" Remember that you are learning to awaken more and more of your sexual potential, and that it is beneficial to your total health and well-being.

Hold the vibrator on the clitoris, or beside the clitoris if this is too sensitive to be pleasurable. Begin to let yourself go and experience the stimulation. Breathe deeply, and relax more and more into the sensation as it builds. If the sensitivity suddenly fades away, reposition the vibrator and continue until it returns. It is helpful to bring to mind any sexual fantasies that are especially erotic to you. This will help you reach an orgasm more quickly, because you are not directly focusing on your physical response. The fantasy helps get your conscious mind out of the way. If your body wants to move or assume different positions, just flow with it. If you have spent years blocking your second chakra, you may need to work with this method for three months or more before you get results. What you are really doing is learning how to relax and feel comfortable with your body. We are naturally orgasmic, and the natural response and pulsation and movement within the sexual organs takes over when we let it. Just be patient with yourself and keep a positive, healthy orientation about the importance of what you are doing. And men should not feel threatened or have any worries about being replaced by a vibrator. There is no substitute for the exchange of energies when making love with your partner. But initially learning to tune into your body and know what feels good to you is often best done alone, especially if you feel embarrassed about masturbating to begin with.

Another method of self-stimulation is to let a stream of water from the bath tub faucet hit the clitoris. After a hot bath let the water out of the tub, place your buttocks beside the open drain, prop your legs up, and turn on the water. This is a highly stimulating and quick way to reach a climax. Of course, you can always use your fingers to manually stimulate yourself, but a vibrator or the water method is less tiring.

Premature ejaculation also results from an imbalance of energy within the chakras, and an inability to regulate its flow throughout the higher centers. To avoid premature ejaculation the man should take deep breaths through his nose, visualizing the energy flowing from his sexual center into his higher chakras. Deep, slow breathing is a very effective technique by itself in determining how long a man can sustain an erection. Also, if a man consistently has an orgasm before his partner, they can make love, wait an hour and then make love again. The second time the man is capable of sustaining an erection much longer. Another method for immediately correcting the unfulfilled woman is to engage in a lot of foreplay where the man stimulates the woman to a climax, lets her relax a moment and experience the sensation, then enters her and continues with the love-making until he also climaxes. All thoughts of fear from both partners should be released from the mind, because if the mind focuses on a negative possibility it tends to follow through on the program.

Nymphomania, incidentally, is the reverse of frigidity. The second chakra is wide open, and the woman hasn't learned to pull the energy up into her higher centers. The energy is so intense that she is unable to control the ebb and flow of the experience and so cannot experience an orgasm.

Any of these problems can be corrected through understanding how energy enlivens or blocks sensitivity in any part of the body. If you have labeled yourself as "frigid" or "impotent" and have decided that you are a poor lover, begin to practice the techniques in this chapter for regulating your energy. Do not allow a negative self-image to deprive you of the pleasure you deserve.

Sharing Your Fantasies

Although many people never reveal that they have sexual fantasies, we all fantasize at some time or another. Sharing your fantasies with your partner can be fun and provide new dimensions to your sexual experience together. Also, looking at your fantasies can give you additional self-insight on how you perceive yourself in a sexual role. For example, if your fantasies usually involve someone dominating you in the sexual act against your will, you may need to develop more of your own masculine side and realize that it is all right for you to give freely when making love. If you are always the dominator, you may need to look at developing your sensitivity and being able to get turned on when receiving love.

Both men and women are able to have orgasms through mental fantasies alone, which suggests to us the power of the mind in triggering sexual receptivity.

Fear of Pregnancy and Birth Control

Another major block to enjoying the sexual experience is the fear of pregnancy. But with birth control methods available today, this should be easily eliminated. My channel states that the vasectomy is the safest and most effective form of birth control, because it does not affect the hormonal balance in the man. Tubal ligations for women are also recommended, but the operation is harder on the woman and takes her longer to recover her energy level. My teachers also recommend using foam or a diaphragm, except in such cases where the individual is too sensitive to the chemicals in the foam or experiences discomfort with the insertion of the diaphragm. Condoms, of course, are a reliable method. However, my channel is very much against the pill, stating that there is too much we do not understand about its effects on the body. Also, they don't recommend the IUD because of the danger involved in puncturing the uterus wall. You should select a method you feel comfortable with, and one that in no way endangers your health.

Techniques for Attunement

The following techniques incorporate relaxation, meditation, visualization and the regulation of breathing. They will help you awaken your sexual awareness and more fully experience both yourself and your partner. Remember that the techniques should be used with an understanding of qualitatively changing your experience, because you are changing yourself and moving into a higher consciousness. Any technique will eventually become boring if you remain on the second chakra level. We must be continuously growing within if our sexual experience remains new and exhilarating. Techniques without love mean nothing.

As you become more sensitive to the life energy, the sexual energy, within, you are awakening yourself physically, mentally and spiritually. An orgasm is a subjective experience, based on where you are at any given moment. There is no such thing as a standard or normal orgasm, just as there is no such thing as a standard religious experience. Each of us experiences and feels in his own way. Emphasis should not be placed solely on achieving an orgasm, because the whole process of opening and sensing is equally important.

Be patient and relax. It takes nine to fourteen years of sensing and balancing energies before the real spiritual blending begins to manifest. But you'll begin experiencing heightened awareness and energy attunement almost as soon as you begin to practice. You are opening yourself to the God force or Love force within you, and this will begin to awaken you to a new life.

Basic orientation and positive suggestions. For you to experience the maximum benefit from the techniques, you must be in a relaxed state with a positive orientation toward both yourself and your partner. Sit comfortably, and begin to focus on your breathing. Tense all the muscles in your body, then relax the tension. Mentally repeat: "My body is relaxed. My mind is relaxed. All experiences, whether physical, mental, emotional or spiritual, are for my learning and growth. I am learning to recognize on every level of my being my oneness with all truth, all joy, all beauty, all love." Continue breathing deeply and rhythmically, relaxing your body and mind more and more. Then give yourself the following positive suggestions (or similar suggestions in your own words): "I delight in my body. Every part of my body is sensitive, beautiful and loving. I delight in my mind. My mind is sensitive, beautiful and loving. My sexual awareness and enjoyment increase day by day. Sexual attunement and harmony with my partner are enhanced day by day. I am free to experience myself and my partner completely, free to enjoy, free to give and receive." Then proceed with any of the following techniques.

Basic tantra technique. This technique, given to me by my channel, was designed particularly for us in the Western world. It is recommended for all sexual imbalances, whether impotence, premature ejaculation, frigidity, or other dysfunction. It begins to unify our physical, mental and spiritual selves. It is a simple process that takes about 40 to 45 minutes, and should be done once every two weeks or at lease once a month. Even if you've been sexually inactive for years, it will begin to awaken your body and restore sexual functioning. The steps are as follows:

1. The woman lies on her back and the man lies at a right angle to her on his left side. The woman puts her right leg between the man's legs, and her left leg over his hip in a scissors position. The penis is inserted in the vagina, whether hard or soft, or if quite flaccid may be gently pressed against the vaginal opening. Both should be comfortable, and the man may wish to put a pillow under his head.

2. No physical movement is made throughout practicing the technique. There is no pressure to perform or to do anything. Both people are just relaxing, attuning, feeling. To begin the process, both partners focus on the genital area. Each visualizes a disc of light encompassing both male and female genitals, which represents the life energy in the second chakra.

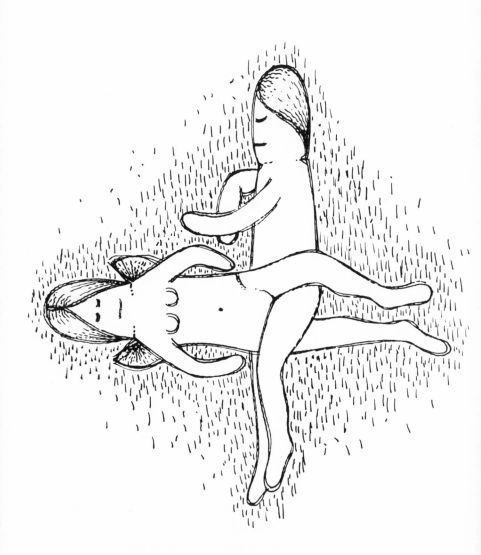

Illustration 2. Basic Tantra Position.

3. Now the male exhales deeply, imagining that he is pushing the light energy from the second chakra up through his partner's body to the crown of her head. At the same time the female inhales deeply, imagining she is pulling the energy up from the sexual center to her crown. Then the male inhales, pulling the energy back from his partner's crown, through their sexual organs, and all the way up to his own crown. Likewise, the female is exhaling and picturing the energy flowing from the crown of her head, through the sexual center, and up to the crown of her partner's head. One is inhaling, the other exhaling, simultaneously, and they are picturing the energy flowing back and forth between them.
4. After picturing the energy flowing back and forth for several minutes, both partners relax the imagery and tune into the feeling in their bodies, entering a meditative state. They continue in this way for about 35-40 more minutes, relaxing, flowing, experiencing.

This technique aligns the seven chakras of the male with the seven chakras of the female, and heightens awareness of each through the combined energies. During the technique the partners may leave the body, their sense of physical awareness, and have the experience of totally merging with the spiritual, emotional and physical dimensions of one another. (It is a oneness with God, a total union.) Usually both are so high and mellow that they go on to sleep. If they want to make love either before or after the technique, fine. But there should be no movement during the 40-45 minutes.

This position can be used just as effectively by homosexuals, and will have the same balancing effect on their energy fields, increasing their love bond.

Remember that learning to love and communicate, sensing deeper levels of awareness within ourselves, is a way of life. There are no instant enlightenment techniques and no free rides. But day by day, we see continuous improvement.

Illustration 3. Tantra Variation.

Tantra variation. Another variation of the tantra technique, depending on your build and inclination, is to sit in a chair face to face with the female on the male's lap, the penis inserted in the vagina. The female may want to put a pillow under her buttocks to take some of her weight off the man's legs. You are holding one another, your spines straight, and you begin the breathing and visualization technique as described in the basic tantra position (101). As one partner inhales, the other exhales, and you pull the energy back and forth between you. Again, there is no physical movement, and you continue in this position for about 40-45 minutes.

Sensing through the hands. This technique is a simple one which helps you tune into your partner's energy through using your hands. There is no performance orientation, and it forces you to move into the subjective realm of experience, opening yourself more fully.

Both partners sit comfortably face to face, holding their hands up together in a patty-cake position. They close their eyes, breathe deeply, and begin to relax. Each should imagine that the only way he or she has of communicating with the other is through sensing the energy in the hands. Each just relaxes and tries to pick up feelings of the other person, and after about three to five minutes they tell each other what they have experienced. Also, with eyes closed they should move their palms away from the partner's hands about two inches, and sense the energy field between their hands. They can practice imagining that the field is growing stronger, then weaker, deliberately controlling the flow of energy between them through their mental orientation.

Sensing through the solar plexus. For this technique each partner lies down, with one's head at the other's feet. Each places his hand on the other's solar plexus, and begins to relax completely and just sense his partner's breathing. Through tuning into the rising and falling of the solar plexus area, each gets a sense of energy flowing through his partner's body, and

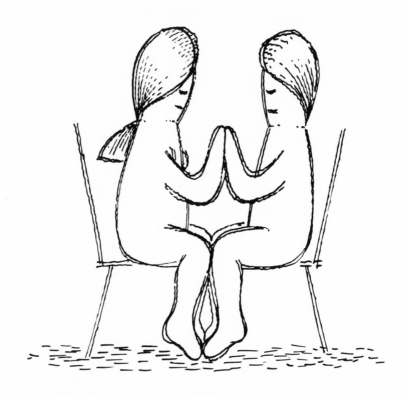

Illustration 4. Sensing through the Hands.

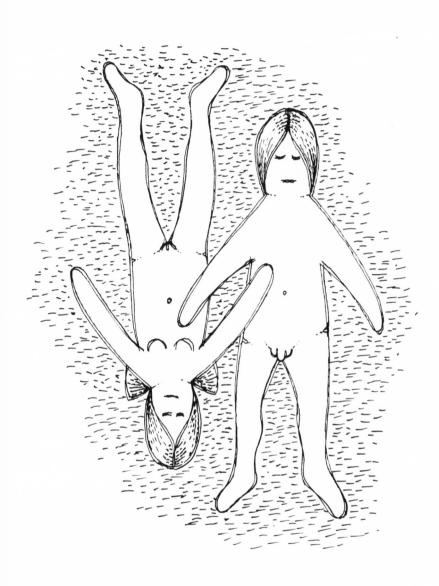

Illustration 5. Sensing through the Solar Plexus.

often is able to determine the degree of tension of the partner. After awhile the breathing of both people may automatically regulate itself together, but neither should consciously try to achieve regulation. After about five to ten minutes both partners should talk about what they experienced, what they felt, their degree of relaxation, how their perception changed as they continued further into the process, whether they were self-conscious, and so on.

Heart chakra tune-in. This is a mental imagery technique which is especially helpful for setting the stage for sensitivity and communication before you begin love-making, or it can be used by itself just to increase your awareness of your own energy field, your partner's energy field, and merging the two together.

1. The partners sit facing one another, spines straight, and palms turned up in their laps. They close their eyes, breathe deeply, and relax the tension in their bodies and minds.
2. Each visualizes a disc of golden light in his own heart chakra, tuning into it, and feeling the energy and warmth.
3. Then each expands the disc of light to include his own energy field, feeling himself completely surrounded in this light, engulfed, and protected.
4. Now each imagines the light expanding to include his own and his partner's energy field, so that the two people are sitting together completely engulfed in a huge sphere of white light energy. Each partner has consciously merged his energy field with that of the other. They should remain in this state for about five minutes, sensing, imagining and experiencing the effect of the combined auras.
5. Then each one returns the light to his own field, then back again to his heart center. (If you are going to make love, begin after step four.)

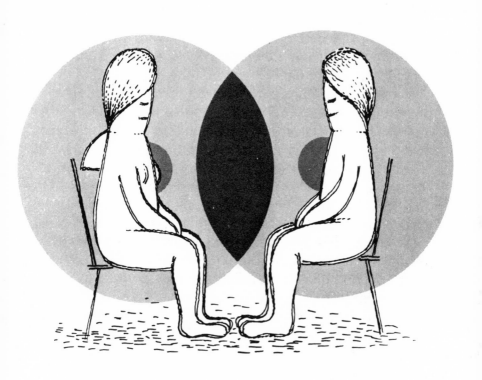

Illustration 6. Heart Chakra Tune-In.

Stimulating the clitoris during sexual intercourse. A woman can learn to have an orgasm when the penis is inserted in the vagina, rather than being manually stimulated or masturbated to climax, but the man must be so positioned that the penis stimulates the clitoris when he thrusts back and forth. The diameter and length of a penis are not particularly important in helping a woman achieve orgasm, rather it is whether he is making contact with the clitoris.

If a man has a long penis, he might prefer to put his legs on the outside of the woman's legs and support himself on his elbows, which allows maximum stimulation for the woman [see Illustration 7(A)]. If the man's penis is short, then he should place his legs on the inside of the woman's legs, the woman spreading her legs apart, knees up and feet flat. The man positions himself on his knees, supporting himself on his elbows or holding his partner [see Illustration 7(B)].

Awakening the sexual center and directing energy. A meditation technique that can be used for awakening energy in the second chakra and directing energy throughout the body is very effective when used once or twice a week. It is especially recommended for the elderly, and those who experience frigidity and impotence. One should sit with spine erect, feet flat on the floor, palms up and relax by breathing deeply and rhythmically. Attention should then be focused on the sexual center, or sexual organs, by picturing a disc of light surrounding and including the genital area. One should endeavor to create a sense of tingling or heat through the visualization. After a few minutes the disc of light should be gently floated up through all the centers, coming to rest on the top of the head. The person then imagines all the centers filled with light, and a stream of energy flowing from the base of the spine to the crown of the head. Regular daily meditation will also help awaken and open the energy centers.

A Word About Sensitivity at Different Times of the Month

We are all familiar with the menstrual cycle of the woman,

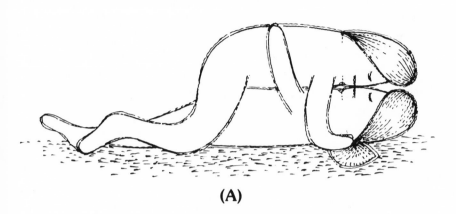

(A)

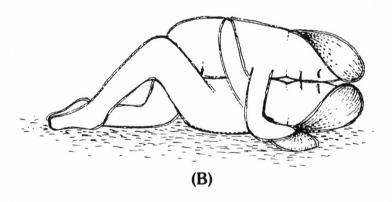

(B)

Illustration 7. Position for Clitoral Stimulation.

and that her interest in and sensitivity to sex varies with the hormonal level of her body. Most of us, however, don't realize that a man also changes in his degrees of responsiveness during the month depending on his hormonal cycles. If you do not feel as high sometimes as you do at others, there is nothing to worry about. It is just the natural fluctuation of your own body chemistry. As we develop more and more of our spiritual consciousness, however, we move beyond the mood variations of body chemistry and elevate ourselves to new levels of responsiveness and joy.

Chapter 6

Meditation: How to Achieve
A Continuous High

Throughout this book I have talked about the value of meditation. There are many different definitions of meditation, and hundreds of techniques are described as the meditation process. Actually, the techniques are as varied as individuals themselves. But what meditation really is must be individually experienced. It is going within and working on yourself, heightening your own energy vibrations. It is a process which helps you get control of your thinking and feeling, and begin to sense an inner Presence or knowing. This Presence is the God-self or Teacher within you, the infinite and unlimited nature of your being.

Quite simply, meditation teaches you how to be your own guru. We are always looking for answers. We read books, go to seminars, talk with people we consider to be wiser than ourselves. People come to me for psychic readings because they think I know something they don't know. I've been meditating for ten years and my intuitional ability is enhanced, and so I have more clarity on some of the numbers they're running. But they could get this same clarity if they wanted to. I encourage people to get their own answers, because every-one of us is psychic and everyone of us has the answer within ourselves to any problem or situation we may be facing. This truth has been taught by spiritual teachers throughout all the ages. Meditation, they have said, is the path to God consciousness. Look within, and you will find all knowledge. But we don't hear it. "Within me?" we question. "You mean I can really find all the answers to problems of life and love within myself?" Our greatest teacher is right inside us.

It is important not to confuse the many techniques of meditation with the inner being you are getting in touch with. Some techniques utilize mantras, some visual symbols, and others incorporate singing and dancing. Some are active and some passive. But all are designed to help you move beyond the present level of your thoughts and habit patterns into an expanded reality.

In your meditation process you are being still, relaxing your awareness of everyday concerns, tuning into deeper dimensions of yourself. You are awakening and bringing up the kundalini energy which will begin to flow throughout all your energy centers. Thus you are heightening and broadening the unseen energy field which exists within and around your body. This is turn raises your physical, mental and spiritual vibrations and serves as a protection so that only higher vibrations can penetrate this field. You can ride the ups and downs of life much easier, because you have gotten in touch with that inner reservoir of strength and well-being.

We are like little light bulbs. If our light bulb is dim, then things around us won't seem to be going well, and we will be more subject to disease and negativity. But when we recharge our light bulbs through meditation, we are able to laugh at things that would normally get us down. Our psychological and physical resistance to negativity is greatly enhanced. It is always our energy level that determines whether things upset us or leave us untouched.

Energy and Schizophrenics

Before I got into meditation I was an introvert. I hid from the world for five years. All I knew was that if I got out in crowds I would get deathly sick, paranoid, and I wanted to run and hide. Also, if I passed someone on the street whose energy was down I would be overcome by depression and wouldn't know where it came from. I didn't know how to tune *out*, to build up my energy field so I wouldn't be picking up everybody else's trips around me.

I've worked with schizophrenics and other mental patients, and for the most part there is nothing wrong with them except they don't know how to tune out the rest of the world. When our energy is low we pick up everyone's fear and negativity, because we don't have that protective field to buffer for us. No one can stay tuned in all the time. In fact, once when I was working with a boy diagnosed as a schizophrenic he asked me, "How come you aren't in here, too, committed like the rest of us?" He knew I was tuning in on him, and that I knew exactly where his head was. I just told him, "Because I know how to control it, and you haven't been willing to learn." He knew that was right on. Anyone can hear voices, and most mental patients who say they hear voices really do. There are plenty of entities and thought waves floating around that we can easily pick up on, and if we're wide open it's like listening to thousands of radio stations at the same time. It makes no sense, and can "drive us crazy." So we must learn how to listen to our own frequency, and tune into others only as we so desire. The ability to tune out other's tensions and pressures gives us a real freedom and better insights into our own trips. This is something that we all must practice as we go through our daily lives.

We can spend years going through psychotherapy, trying to analyze our behavior and discover reasons why we are unhappy. We can spend years trying to understand the games our parents and friends have run on us.

And even if you clear out a lot of the old hang-ups through a process of counseling or psychotherapy, and then another traumatic event happens in your life and throws you all out of kilter again, what have you really learned? Through heightening your energy and learning the attitude of meditation you establish a new approach to living. You are developing a way of creative problem solving, realizing that everything that happens is for your growth, and you have a relaxed and joyous orientation toward things you come into contact with. We must learn to live effectively in the present, in addition to releasing our past blocks.

Prayer, Dreams and Meditation

There are only three tools that we need to get through life: dreams, prayer and meditation. Dreams give us an immediate symbolic read-out on our attitudes and how we are handling our daily lives; prayer enables us to formulate clear images in our minds of what we really want, what our goals are; and meditation helps us to be still and listen to the God-force within us.

It is said that prayer is talking to God, and meditation is listening. Most of us talk but we never sit still long enough to listen and hear the answer. Meditation is attuning to the force that unites us with all life, that takes us beyond our immediate needs and concerns and gives us a more universal perspective in expanded levels of consciousness.

Meditation — Not a Religion

Meditation is not a religion, but it can enrich any faith. All religions are good, and God doesn't care what you believe. The key is whether you are learning how to love, and recognizing the God-force within all people. The heart of all great religious teachings is that God is love, although dogma and tradition have tended to block that message.

You don't have to consider yourself a "religious person" to meditate. You can be an atheist or agnostic, anything you like. But probably you'll grant that every person is in some way an expression or result of a cosmic process or creative force. We know that energy is indestructible, and that science is beginning to believe the universe is more like an alive organism than a purposeless machine. Meditation is a way to contact the cosmic process or universal energy that is responsible for you as an expression of life. You may call this process what you like. I call it God. And when you meditate you align yourself with God, which is the most powerful force in the universe.

My personal belief is in Jesus, because I was raised a Baptist. But the Christ spirit is the love spirit within all people, and I'll listen to Buddha or any other teacher who has something to teach me. Truth is where you find it, my channel has often said. You may be given an eternal truth from the beggar on the street as readily as in a special vision. But whenever it comes we must have the ears to hear and the eyes to see.

A Vision

I had a vision several years ago. I was standing on top of a mountain with an oriental teacher. He said to me, "Look down at the bottom of the mountain." There were millions of people, and they looked like little ants because they were so far away. Some were walking around in circles, some were climbing up steep cliffs, and others were plodding along fairly easy terrain. The teacher said to me, "One day all people will reach the top of the mountain, and it matters not how they get here. It doesn't matter what path they walk. Each one ultimately must learn to know himself and the God within him." He explained that God is very patient, and we have an eternity to learn. In other words, follow the path that feels right for you and don't put down the way another has chosen.

The Meditation Technique

The process of meditation is easy to learn. (It is practicing the insights of love and truth in your daily life that is difficult.) No matter what your personal beliefs or your present level of awareness, meditation will begin an unfolding *within* at the level that is right for you.

This meditation technique was given to me by my channel, and is an ancient Egyptian method. It is divided into two parts,

Illustration 8. Concentration Position. Spine erect, feet flat on floor, hands together, eyes opened or closed.

including both concentration and meditation. It is very simple, yet highly effective.

Remember that any meditation technique is good, but no matter what you use it is important to close down at the end of your meditation period. This involves closing your palms into fists, and imagining a huge ball of white light completely surrounding you. This protects your heightened sensitivity, and does not leave you wide open to other people's negative energy. Unfortunately, most meditation schools do not teach the process of closing down, and many people report that they begin to feel irritated after they have been meditating for a few months, which is a result of leaving themselves wide open.

The following technique takes twenty minutes a day, which is enough to recharge your energy field for the next twenty-four hours. Remember that it is best not to meditate on a full stomach or when you are overly tired, but that any time is better than no time at all.

Sit in a straight-backed chair, with your spine erect, feet flat on the floor, and hands resting in prayer position or gently folded together in your lap. (Or if you prefer sit cross-legged on the floor in lotus position). Imagine yourself completely surrounded in white light energy, breathe deeply, and relax. The first ten minutes is concentration, and your eyes may be opened or closed. Concentration is simply the focusing of your mind on a single point. It clears away the mental cobwebs, stills the active conscious mind, and directs your energy. If you prefer to leave your eyes open, fix your gaze on a single object or symbol, something that suggests harmony, beauty, or balance. If you wish to concentrate with your eyes closed, visualize a peaceful outdoor scene, an inspiring word (such as love, peace, or joy), a religious symbol, or anything else that is highly inspirational and uplifting to you. You may wish to listen to uplifting music, or to repeat mantras or verses from religious scriptures. It doesn't matter, as long as you are centering your thoughts. Whenever your thoughts stray from

Illustration 9. Meditation Position. Spine erect, feet flat on floor, palms open, eyes closed.

your object of focus, simply bring them back again. Do not be concerned if your mind wanders frequently. Be very patient and gently return your thoughts to your object of focus each time you realize you have wandered off.

After about ten minutes of disciplining your mind to stay centered on one thing, you then gently shift into the meditation period for the second ten minutes. Turn your palms up, which allows for maximum energy flow through your body, and if your eyes were opened, close them. You now let the mind you have been disciplining relax. Don't try to control or focus your thoughts. Make no conscious effort to think about anything. Just set your mind free. Thoughts and mental images may cross your mind. Examine them placidly as they come and go. You may "see" colors or beautiful scenes, be filled with inspiration, or just stare at the backs of your eyelids. It doesn't matter; just be still, detached, and flow with whatever you are experiencing.

You may feel slight chills, vibrations along your spine, sensations of coolness on your skin. You may feel your body growing quite hot, or lose awareness of your body altogether. Again, note any such sensations with calm, relaxed interest. You are heightening your senses of your total being and are more receptive to the finer energy forces around you. If you feel dizzy, nauseous, or get a headache, it is probably resulting from too much energy pouring into your body. Bring your thumb and index finger together and this will slow down the energy flow. Remember, you are in control of your experiences. If you experience anything you don't like or want, just say, "The energy is now easing off," quietly directing it to pour through your system more slowly.

You may feel the energy moving throughout your body as tingling or a mild electrical current. Imagine it rising up to the crown of your head from the base of your spine, flowing smoothly and rhythmically throughout your entire system. Often people get sexually aroused when they start meditating, and begin to fantasize and forget that they were supposed to be meditating in the first place. The sexual turn on, as I mentioned earlier, occurs because the kundalini energy is coming up and hitting the second chakra, and this happens whether you are 16 or 106. Don't let this upset you. Just imagine a disc of light in the second chakra, and then picture it moving up into your higher centers, up to the top of your head. This is similar to the technique given in Chapter 5 to awaken and balance the sexual energy. As you begin to move the energy higher in your body, the sexual sensitivity will subside, that is, until you deliberately create it again by directing energy to the second center.

After about ten minutes of meditation close your palms, imagine a luminous white light completely surrounding you, then open your eyes. The circle of light should have at least an eight foot diameter so that it completely engulfs you and extends into your aura or energy field. This closes down the centers which have been opened during the meditation process and protects you from outside influences. This does not close you off from other people, however. What you are doing is protecting yourself from being affected by any negativity and at the same time radiating love and harmony to those around you. This white light is a real and dynamic force. You may use it not only in conjunction with your meditation, but at any time during the day when you feel your energy is low or you're in a negative mind-set.

The concentration and meditation technique may be easily summarized into seven steps:

1. Sit in a straight backed chair with spine erect, feet flat on the floor. Fold your hands together in your lap, or hold them in prayer position. Eyes may be opened or closed.
2. Take several deep breaths, and feel yourself relaxing. Imagine a bright white light completely surrounding you, which is your protection as you open sensitive energy centers.
3. Gently concentrate on a single idea, picture or word for about ten minutes. Select something that suggests

peace, beauty, or a spiritual ideal; or just listen to soft, soothing music.

4. If your mind strays from your object of concentration, gently bring it back to your focal point. (Surprisingly soon you'll find your ability to discipline the mind growing much stronger.)

5. After 10 minutes separate your hands and turn them palms up in your lap. Close your eyes if opened.

6. Relax your hold on the concentration object, and shift your mind into neutral. Remain passive yet alert for ten minutes. Placidly observe any thoughts and images as they may come and go. Just be still, detached, and flow with whatever you are experiencing.

7. After 10 minutes open your eyes, close your palms, and again imagine that you are surrounded completely by a white light. This is your continued protection as you go about your daily activities.

This twenty minute period is recharging your energy field. But we should practice the meditation attitude, watching our responses, thoughts and behavior, throughout each day. Meditation is not an escape from life, but a process that enables us to be involved more fully by seeing how we are setting up our own experiences. Sometimes the changes we experience are dramatic, sometimes subtle. But meditation will change your life, because it changes you.

Understanding Negativity Sometimes Experienced in Meditation

When you begin meditating your growth is being accelerated. But we don't always understand that what is happening to us is for our good. We may see and hear things during meditation that are negative and we may begin to believe that something is terribly wrong.

Sometimes people will stop meditating after awhile because of this. But it is just their own inner garbage that has finally been loosened up enough to surface for them to look at. We all have this negativity, buried self-destruct tendencies, and we simply must let it come up and out. If you hear a voice that tells you to do something that would be harmful to yourself or others, just mentally say, "No thanks, I don't need it," and let the thoughts float right out of your mind.

The key to successful growth in meditation is detachment from whatever you are experiencing, as mentioned when describing the technique. Meditation channels energy through your physical, mental and emotional being and releases anything that you have suppressed, anything that limits your total state of harmony. If you think something "evil" is in your consciousness, it is probably the result of some experience or feeling you suppressed a long time ago and had forgotten all about. The only workable attitude when such thoughts and images pass through your mind is "Gee, how interesting. I didn't know that was in there. Glad I discovered it so now I can release it."

If you don't want to learn to know yourself, if you don't want to grow, if you don't want to clear out your inner blocks, then don't start meditating. It's fine to feel great elation and spiritual renewal during your meditation period, but in order to maintain those highs on a continuous basis, we have to release the limiting programs that block us from knowing our true spiritual nature 24 hours a day. But if we realize what is happening, and know how to handle the unpleasantness, it doesn't seem negative at all. Rather we have an attitude of thankfulness that we've finally gotten in touch with a deeper level of our own subconscious mind.

My channel has said that the primary causes of physical and mental illness are guilt, fear, and lack of self-worth. Out of these grow hatred, anger, and condemnation of ourselves and others. We must be willing to release these feelings from our minds, and we cannot afford to suppress them, or else we will become sick. We must let them go by learning to identify with the God-self within us.

When we begin to develop the attitude of detachment from

thoughts and experiences, we really begin to know the Presence that transcends all thought, all things. We realize that there are no obstacles we cannot overcome, and we discover the strength and courage to deal with any situation in our lives, minus the usual accompanying fear, and so we are able to move quickly through it.

Your teachers will never lead you into a situation that you cannot handle or that you aren't ready for. Because you have free will you can chose not to look at it, not to see the lesson. And this will result in your feeling confused and frustrated. Because the energy is so high at this particular time on the earth plane we have the opportunity to look at and eliminate many of our negative programs. All those insecurity feelings, grudges, fears, and annoyances we can let go. So when they come up, whether in the waking state or in your meditation, just remember to say "thanks."

Meditation and Celibacy

In the ancient esoteric cults people were taught at a very young age how to channel the kundalini energy into the higher centers and use it as heightened intuitional awareness. They learned how to direct and balance the energy through meditation, and practiced a life of celibacy to maintain a high peak of control. The idea that sexual intercourse interfered with spiritual development has been carried over to our present day, but with the lack of knowledge possessed by the ancient orders.

Priests and nuns are asked to take the vow of chastity, but for the most part they are unprepared spiritually for what this actually means. Meditation does channel the life energy into higher centers, but to really pull off the celibacy trip one would have to have meditated for many years, and have an advanced understanding of the kundalini force in order not to experience any negative effects. In our culture we really do not need to practice celibacy to become enlightened. I've counseled many priests and nuns who felt guilty because they had turned to masturbation, simply because they were so frustrated and didn't know how to handle the energy. I tell them that it's perfectly all right to masturbate, and that this force is very real and that it takes many years of working with it to be able to gain complete control and not suppress in any of our chakras.

Some of the modern cults which are offshoots of Eastern religious groups are teaching their followers to adhere to a celibate life. I've worked with young couples who have had a very difficult time in their marriages because their guru had told them to have sexual intercourse only once a month. It plays havoc with their health, even if they are meditating, and leads to prostate problems.

Another spin-off on the relationship of meditation and celibacy is the teaching that one loses sexual desire after a number of years of meditating, and this is a mark of becoming more spiritual. If we accept the programming that "Lack of sexual desire means increased spirituality," we will probably begin to let our sexual orientation dwindle, and for no really good reason other than it is supposed to be a sign of our enlightenment.

A woman told me that she had been meditating for a number of years, and because of this she was no longer interested in having sex with her husband. The husband was trying to renew their sexual relationship to no avail. She was confident that she had raised her level of consciousness to a point where she didn't need sex. When she attended a religious meeting later on she suddenly found herself sexually attracted to another man, which greatly surprised her. She was discovering that her sexual energy was very much alive, and that she had not been looking at problems in the marital relationship that needed to be worked out. There was more to rejecting her husband than she had wanted to look at.

None of us can finish his earthly incarnations celibate. It's easy to love the masses when we aren't emotionally involved. But our true test comes in the one-to-one relationship when we get all our buttons pushed into jam! We have to look at all our positive and negative programs so we can sift through the limiting beliefs and attitudes we have acquired over lifetimes.

When we begin to open and balance all the chakras through meditation, we see each one as an equally potent expression of the God-force. We are no longer controlled or dominated by any one of them, but are free to choose to experience the world through any or all chakras. We can delight in our sex life as well as in our creative projects and intuitive awareness.

Perhaps the most helpful thing is to realize that celibacy is much more a mind state than a physical practice. If we remain married to our higher consciousness, and unmarried to our lower consciousness, we are achieving a union with God. My channel has stressed that whether one lives in a state of physical chastity is unimportant in the present age, but rather it is how an individual develops his own talents and God-given abilities.

Meditation as a Way of Life

Meditation is a way of life that you cultivate over the years. It takes time and diligence, just as developing your inter-personal relationships takes time and diligence. Combining meditation techniques with techniques for building harmony with your partner encourages the fastest growth in the parti-cular age we are living in.

It is in the inner stillness of your being that you realize the direction for your life, gain understanding of yourself, and know the meaning of Love. It is through this inner stillness that you are able to merge and become one with yourself, with another, and with God.

Dare to look inside and find out what you really are. The love, beauty and joy you will discover is greater than you ever imagined possible.